Reported, Then Blamed

Institutional Betrayal, the DARVO Reversal, and How to Reclaim Yourself When the Organization Turned Its Harm Into Your Fault

Arnold Wellington McLean

The DARVO Survival Guides, Book 5

Copyright

First Edition

ISBN: 979-8-90678-198-7

Staten House

Table of Contents

Preface

Over the past decade, research on how organizations respond to reports of wrongdoing has given a name to an experience that many people once suffered without one. When someone reports harm, misconduct, or a safety concern to an institution they depend on, and the institution protects itself by turning on the person who reported, the injury has a shape that scholars have begun to map. The concept of institutional betrayal, developed in the psychological literature, describes the harm a body does when it fails or turns on those who rely on it for safety. Yet the specific tactic by which institutions accomplish this reversal, and the toll it takes on the individual, has received far less direct treatment in books written for the people living through it.

That tactic is called DARVO, an acronym for deny, attack, and reverse victim and offender. It names a sequence in which the party confronted denies the wrongdoing, attacks the credibility and character of the person who named it, and reverses the roles until the reporter becomes the accused. It is worth distinguishing from a fair process that reaches an unwelcome conclusion in good faith on reasonable grounds. What sets the reversal apart is that the response to being held accountable is to relocate the fault onto the reporter, and in an institution this relocation can be carried out by many people at once, clothed in the language of procedure.

The difficulty for the person turned on by an institution is that they often cannot tell whether they got it wrong or were reversed. Such a reader tends to read their own reaction to being mishandled as the offense, to defer to the institution's confident account over their own record, and to face the reversal without a clear way to weigh it. What is usually missing is not sympathy but a method, and a way to protect the self while the institution insists that self is the problem.

This book supplies both. It applies the DARVO framework to the institution and follows it through the structures that sustain it: the shifting of the subject from the wrong to the reporter, the gaslighting, the closing of ranks, the prolonged process. It provides a fair self-check for telling a genuine mistake a reader should own from a false frame they should refuse, a way to read an institution by the direction of its power rather than the politeness of its procedures, and a framework for deciding whether to stay, leave, or pursue the matter. The aim is a reader who can keep their bearings and rebuild a self grounded in evidence.

Reported, Then Blamed is the fifth book in The DARVO Survival Guides. The earlier volumes address the reversal in adult relationships, in divorce and custody, in friendships and the workplace, and in the family of origin. This one turns to the institution, and it can be read on its own or alongside the others.

The book is written first for the person who reported a wrong to an organization and was recast as the problem. It will also be useful to the advocates, lawyers, and clinicians who support such readers. It is not therapy, and it is not legal advice, and anyone facing a formal or legal process should seek qualified counsel. It cannot determine the facts of any situation or institution, and it promises no particular outcome. What it offers is a clear way to understand one of the most disorienting experiences a working adult can face, and a practical path back to a self worth trusting.

Introduction: You Turned to Them for Help

You did what you were supposed to do. You saw something wrong, or something wrong was done to you, and you reported it to the people whose job was to handle it. You went to human resources, or the compliance office, or the university's Title office, or the professional body, or the church leadership, or the regulator, trusting that an organization built to address exactly this would address it. And then, somewhere in the process, the ground shifted under you. The problem stopped being the thing you reported and started being you. Your credibility was questioned, your record was combed for faults, your motives were examined, and within weeks or months you found yourself the subject of the inquiry you thought you had started. The institution you turned to for help had turned on you.

This book is about that reversal, and about the fact that it has a name and a shape. When a person is confronted about harm, or when the wrongdoing they report threatens an organization's interests, the response is often not to address the harm but to turn the whole thing around. The harm is denied. The person who named it is attacked, their credibility and character put on trial. And the roles are reversed, so that the one who reported becomes the one accused, the problem to be managed, the threat to be contained. The psychologist Jennifer Freyd called this pattern deny, attack, and reverse victim and offender (Freyd, 1997). When an institution does it to someone who depended on it, the injury is compounded, because the very body you trusted to protect you becomes a second source of harm, distinct from and often worse than the first (Smith & Freyd, 2014).

I want to be careful and clear from the first page, because two very different readers may be holding this book. Most people who reach for a book like this reported something real and were then recast as the problem for reporting it, and everything here is written for them. But it is also possible to have reported something mistakenly, or to have handled a real situation in a way that caused genuine problems, and no truthful book about institutions can skip past that. So this book does not begin by assuring you that you were entirely right. It begins, in an early chapter, by helping you ask the hard question plainly and answer it fairly, because a person of conscience deserves a real method rather than a comforting slogan. If some of what the institution says has truth in it, you will find a way to own that here without accepting a false whole. And if, as is far more likely for a reader who has carried this so carefully, the accusation is a reversal, you will find a way to see it clearly and to set the false role down.

Here is the road ahead. We begin with how institutional betrayal works, how a body you depended on comes to protect itself by turning on you, and how the reversal operates at the organizational level. Then we face the question of whether you got it wrong, with a fair self-check, and we look at institutional gaslighting and why your own record is the ground you stand on. We learn to read an institution by power and direction rather than by its polished procedures and language. We prepare for colleagues and committees closing ranks, and learn why people side with the organization. We learn to answer a process calmly and to release the hope that the institution will one day admit what it did. We turn toward the people who still stand with you, we learn to survive a prolonged investigation without collapsing or exploding, and we learn to own any genuine mistake while refusing the institution's frame. We make a clear, values-based decision about whether to stay, leave, or pursue the matter further. And we finish by rebuilding a self and a working life after the institution turned on you.

This book will not tell you to quit, to sue, or to stay silent, and it will not shame you for any of those choices. It cannot determine the facts of your particular situation, and it promises no specific outcome. What it offers is a clear and rigorous way to think through one of the most disorienting experiences a working adult can face: being recast as the problem by the institution you trusted to do the right thing. You turned to them for help. Their turning on you was not the measure of your worth. Let us begin.

Chapter 1: You Depended on Them

Avelis reported the safety violations because she believed the company would want to know. She was forty, a respected engineer with fifteen years at the firm, and when she found that a supervisor had been signing off on inspections that had never happened, she did the thing she had been trained to do: she documented it and took it to management and then, when management did nothing, to the compliance office. She expected the problem to be the falsified inspections. Instead, within two months, the problem was Avelis. She was described in meetings as difficult, as someone with a grudge against her supervisor, as not a team player. Her past performance reviews, uniformly strong, were suddenly reread for evidence of a pattern. She was moved to a lesser role, described as a lateral change. And she sat in her car one evening and could not understand how she, who had reported the wrongdoing, had become the wrongdoer in the eyes of the only body that could have set it right.

This chapter is about that experience, and about the particular injury of being turned on by an institution you depended on. When you report harm or wrongdoing to an organization, you are not approaching a neutral party. You are approaching a body you rely on for your livelihood, your standing, your safety, or your sense of belonging, and that dependence is exactly what makes the betrayal so devastating when the organization protects itself instead of you. Understanding that what happened to you is a recognized pattern, with a name and a shape, is the first step out of the confusion, because a betrayal you can name is one you can begin to think about clearly rather than only suffer.

You depended on them

The principle of this chapter is that the depth of the betrayal comes from the depth of your dependence. Institutional betrayal is the harm done when an organization that people rely on for safety or wellbeing fails to protect them, or actively harms them, especially after they report a wrong (Smith & Freyd, 2014). The reason it cuts so deeply is the dependence. You did not report to a stranger; you reported to your employer, your school, your hospital, your professional body, your faith community, the institution woven into your daily life and your future. When that body turns on you, it is not only a bad outcome. It is a betrayal by something you needed, and the need is what gives the wound its size.

This dependence is also why the betrayal is so disorienting. A person harmed by a stranger knows where they stand; a person harmed by the institution they trusted has the ground pulled out from under them, because the thing that was supposed to be the solution has become the source of the harm. You may find yourself unable to make sense of it, returning again and again to the question of how this could have happened, and that bewilderment is not a sign that you have misjudged the situation. It is the predictable effect of being betrayed by a body you depended on, which the mind struggles to hold because it violates the basic expectation that the institution was on your side.

The reversal at the institutional level

What turns institutional failure into the specific crisis that brought you here is the reversal, the way the organization does not merely fail to help but actively recasts you as the problem. Confronted with a report that threatens its interests, its reputation, its liability, its comfort, an institution often responds with the pattern named in the introduction: it denies the wrongdoing, attacks the credibility and character of the person who reported, and reverses the roles so that the reporter becomes the accused (Freyd, 1997). The wrong you named recedes, and you move to the center of the inquiry. The question stops being what happened and becomes what is wrong with you.

This is why the accusation feels so total and so strange at once. You came forward about a specific wrong, and now you are defending your whole character, your motives, your history, your temperament. The content has shifted entirely, from the thing you reported to the question of who you are, and this shift is not incidental. It is the reversal working exactly as it works, relocating the fault from the institution onto the person who named it. Seeing that the shift is the tactic, not a fair response to something you did, is a relief, because it means you are not facing a legitimate examination of your defects. You are facing a known move, one that recasts reporters as problems precisely so the institution need not face what was reported.

Why institutions protect themselves

It helps to understand why institutions do this, because the reasons make the reversal predictable rather than mysterious, and predictability takes away some of its power to bewilder. An institution is not a person; it is a system with interests, and its strongest interest is usually self-preservation. A report of wrongdoing threatens the institution with liability, embarrassment, cost, and disruption, and the cheapest way to make that threat disappear is often to discredit the person who raised it rather than to address the wrong. This is not always a conscious conspiracy. It is frequently the sum of many people each protecting the organization, and themselves, by treating the reporter as the problem, because that is the path of least resistance for everyone whose comfort depends on the institution being fine.

Seeing this clears away a painful misunderstanding. When the institution turns on you, it is tempting to conclude that you must have done something to deserve it, because surely a whole organization would not turn on someone without cause. But an organization does not need cause to protect itself; it needs only a threat to its interests, and your report was that threat. The turning was not a considered judgment on your character reached by fair-minded people weighing the evidence. It was a system defending itself in the way systems do, and understanding that is what lets you stop searching your own conduct for the crime that would explain treatment that was never really about your conduct at all. Avelis eventually understood that the firm had not turned on her because she was difficult; it had turned on her because she was inconvenient, and the label of difficult had been applied afterward, to make the turning look justified.

Why it is not your fault that you did not see it coming

Many people in your position torment themselves with a further question: how did I not see this coming, why did I trust them, why did I put myself in this position. This self-blame is worth addressing directly, because it is both common and unfair. You did not see it coming because you were operating on a reasonable and decent assumption, that an institution built to handle wrongdoing would handle it, that reporting a wrong was the right thing to do and would be treated as such. That assumption is not naivety; it is the assumption the institution actively encourages, through its policies, its training, its stated values, its open-door language. You trusted the institution to be what it said it was, and the betrayal is the institution's, not the failure of your trust.

This matters because the reversal is helped along by your self-blame. If you can be made to feel that you were foolish to report, that you should have known better, that you brought this on yourself by speaking up, then you carry part of the institution's fault for it. Setting that down is part of seeing clearly. You did the right thing by reporting, and the fact that the institution punished you for it is a report on the institution, not on your judgment in trusting it. Avelis had believed that reporting the falsified inspections was simply what a responsible engineer did, and she had been right; the failure was not in her decision to report but in an organization that punished the reporting instead of fixing what she reported.

The many forms of the same pattern

It is worth seeing that this pattern is not confined to one kind of institution, because recognizing its reach helps you understand that what happened to you is structural rather than particular to your bad luck. The same reversal runs in a corporation that recasts a whistleblower as a disgruntled employee, a university that turns a student who reported an assault into a disciplinary case, a hospital that treats a nurse who raised safety concerns as the difficult one, a faith community that casts the person who named an abuser as the divisive troublemaker, and a professional body that investigates the member who filed a complaint. The settings differ, the language differs, but the shape is the same: a body that people depend on protects itself by turning on the person who reported a wrong.

Understanding the pattern's reach matters because it corrects the sense that your situation is uniquely yours, uniquely your fault, or uniquely inexplicable. It is none of those. It is a recognizable pattern that has been documented across many kinds of institutions, which means the explanation for what happened to you lies in how institutions behave under threat, not in some special defect in you or some special malice aimed at you personally. Avelis had felt that her situation was a bizarre one-off, a strange thing that had happened to her because of some mistake she must have made. Learning that engineers, nurses, students, and congregants across countless organizations had been through the identical reversal did not undo her injury, but it moved the explanation from her supposed defects to the predictable conduct of institutions, which was where it belonged.

The compounding of two injuries

There is a specific reason institutional betrayal wounds so deeply, and naming it helps you understand why you may be more devastated than the original wrong by itself would account for. When you are harmed and then betrayed by the institution you turned to about the harm, you suffer two injuries, not one, and the second often outweighs the first. The original wrong was painful, but the institution's turning on you added a second and distinct injury: the discovery that the body you relied on for protection would sacrifice you to protect itself. This second betrayal, by a trusted institution, produces harm beyond the original event, and it is frequently the part that people find hardest to recover from (Smith & Freyd, 2014).

This is why you should not measure your devastation against the original wrong and conclude that you are overreacting. The original wrong is only half of what happened to you. The other half is the betrayal by the institution, and that betrayal touches something foundational, the expectation that the systems we depend on will not turn on us when we need them, which is part of how people are able to function in a world full of institutions. When that expectation is shattered, the effect reaches beyond the specific case into a more general loss of trust, and grieving that larger loss, rather than minimizing it, is part of an accurate response. Avelis found that what kept her awake was not mainly the falsified inspections but the memory of the compliance officer's face as he explained her lateral move, the moment she understood that the system had chosen itself over her, and that this second wound was the one she would have to heal.

What this book can and cannot do

One clarification belongs at the start, because it shapes how you should read everything that follows. This book cannot determine the facts of your particular case, and it is not a substitute for the legal and professional help that many institutional situations require. If you are facing a formal investigation, a disciplinary process, or possible legal action, a qualified lawyer or advocate who knows your jurisdiction is a resource this book cannot replace, and seeking one early is often wise. What this book offers is the part that the legal and procedural guides tend to leave out: a way to understand the psychological reversal, to keep your bearings while it is happening, to weigh your own conduct fairly, and to protect and rebuild your sense of who you are while an institution insists you are the problem.

Holding that distinction clearly will serve you throughout. The practical and legal dimension of an institutional matter is real and important, and it is not the subject of this book; the psychological and personal dimension is just as real, often less well served, and it is exactly what these chapters address. You can pursue proper legal advice and also do the inner work of not being defined by the institution's account, and the two support each other, because a person who understands the reversal and holds their bearings is far better placed to make sound practical decisions than one who has been pulled under by the confusion and self-doubt the reversal produces.

Trying it on your own situation

Begin to see the reversal as a recognized pattern.

First, write down, in one or two sentences, what you originally reported. State the wrong itself, plainly, before the reversal moved the subject to you. Naming the original report is how you keep hold of what this was actually about.

Second, write down how the subject shifted. Note the point at which the inquiry stopped being about the wrong you reported and started being about you, your credibility, your motives, your character. Seeing the shift on paper is how you recognize the reversal as a move rather than a fair response.

Third, name the dependence. Write down what you relied on this institution for: your livelihood, your standing, your safety, your belonging. Naming the dependence is how you understand the size of the betrayal, so you can stop treating your devastation as an overreaction to a mere workplace dispute.

Fourth, separate the two injuries. On one line, write the original wrong you reported. On another, write the second injury, the institution's turning on you for reporting it. Keeping them separate helps you see that your devastation is a response to both, and that the second, the betrayal by a body you depended on, is often the larger of the two and the one that will take the most care to heal.

What to carry forward

The depth of the betrayal comes from the depth of your dependence, because institutional betrayal is the harm done when a body you rely on for safety or wellbeing turns on you instead of protecting you (Smith & Freyd, 2014), and the dependence is what gives the wound its size. The reversal at the institutional level recasts you from reporter to accused through the same pattern of deny, attack, and reverse, so the inquiry stops being about the wrong you named and becomes about who you are (Freyd, 1997). Institutions do this because they are systems whose strongest interest is self-preservation, and discrediting the reporter is often cheaper than addressing the wrong, which means the turning was not a fair judgment on your character but a system defending itself. It is not your fault that you did not see it coming, because you trusted the institution to be what it said it was, and that trust was reasonable and decent. Having seen the reversal for what it is, the next chapter looks at how your report, and your reaction to being mishandled, became the evidence against you.

Chapter 2: The Complaint Became the Crime

Caelis sent one frustrated email, and it became the entire case against him. He was forty-three, a hospital nurse who had raised concerns about staffing levels that he believed were putting patients at risk, and for months he had raised them properly, through the channels, in measured language, to no effect. Then one night, after a shift in which a patient nearly came to harm because there were too few staff, he sent an email to his manager that was sharper than his usual tone, a single line saying that if something was not done, the blood would be on management's hands. It was intemperate, and he knew it. And that one email, lifted out of the months of measured concern that preceded it, became the thing the hospital pointed to. Not the staffing crisis he had reported, but his email. He was described as threatening, as unprofessional, as the real problem on the ward. The complaint he had raised vanished from the conversation, and the crime became the way he had raised it.

This chapter is about that transformation, the way the institution makes your report, or your reaction to being ignored and mishandled, into the offense. It is one of the cruelest features of the institutional reversal: everything the wrongdoing recedes, and your conduct in reporting it moves to the center. Your frustration, your persistence, your sharp email, your emotional reaction to being dismissed, all of it is collected and displayed as evidence that you were the problem all along. Learning to see this transformation for what it is, and to keep the original wrong from disappearing behind your reaction to it, is how you stop handing the institution the case it wants to make.

The complaint became the crime

The principle of this chapter is that the institution converts your complaint, and your reaction, into the offense. When an organization does not want to address what you reported, one of its most effective moves is to shift all attention to how you reported it. Suddenly the subject is your tone, your persistence, your temper, your supposed insubordination or unprofessionalism, and the wrong you named is nowhere to be found. This is not a fair response to a real problem with your conduct. It is a redirection, and it works because your conduct in reporting, especially any frustrated or emotional moment, is visible and easy to point to, while the wrong you reported is often diffuse, contested, or concealed.

This redirection is a close cousin of the reactive-defense trap that runs through these situations. When you are harmed or ignored, you react, and the reaction can be seized upon as though it were the origin of the trouble rather than a response to it. A sharp email sent after months of being dismissed is a reaction to being dismissed, not evidence that you were always difficult, but the institution presents it stripped of everything that produced it. Seeing the redirection clearly is what lets you refuse to accept your reaction as the real subject, and to keep pointing, at least in your own mind, back to the wrong that the redirection is designed to bury.

Why your reaction is such useful ammunition

It helps to understand why your reaction is so useful to the institution, because understanding it removes some of the shame that keeps you agreeing with the case against you. A single sharp or emotional moment is vivid, concrete, and easy to document, while the pattern of being ignored, dismissed, and mishandled that produced it is diffuse and hard to point to. Negative and dramatic impressions form quickly and lodge deeply, far more readily than the slow accumulation of small institutional failures (Baumeister et al., 2001). So your one intemperate email is remembered and quoted with perfect clarity, while the months of legitimate concern that led to it leave no single vivid image, and the contest of impressions is rigged from the start.

This asymmetry is why you cannot win by proving your reaction was justified. The reaction photographs; the provocation does not. The email is there as a document; the months of being stonewalled are not any single thing anyone can hold up. Recognizing this changes your strategy: you stop trying to make your reaction look reasonable, which keeps the reaction at the center where the institution wants it, and you work instead to keep the original wrong in view and to place your reaction accurately, as a response within a pattern rather than the origin of it. Caelis spent weeks tormented by his one email, until he understood that the email's vividness was exactly why the hospital had seized on it, and that no amount of explaining the staffing crisis would ever be as memorable as that one sharp line, which meant the contest over the email was one he was never going to win and did not need to fight.

The professional-conduct trap

Institutions have a particular tool for this redirection, and it is worth naming because it is so effective: the language of professionalism and conduct. The wrong you reported gets reframed as a matter of your professional conduct, your communication style, your failure to follow the proper process, your attitude. This reframing is powerful because it sounds neutral and reasonable, even high-minded, and because almost anyone who has been ignored and dismissed for months will eventually do something that can be described as a conduct issue: raise their voice, send a sharp message, go outside the chain, show visible frustration. The institution then treats that conduct issue as the matter at hand, and the original wrong becomes a mere backdrop to your unprofessional behavior.

The trap is that you cannot fully comply your way out of it, because the standard is applied selectively and the bar moves. Report calmly and you are ignored; report persistently and you are aggressive; react emotionally after being dismissed and you are unprofessional; go outside the channel after the channel failed and you are insubordinate. The conduct frame is available to be applied to almost any way you might have reported, because its purpose is not to hold you to a fair standard but to relocate the subject from the institution's wrong to your behavior. Seeing this lets you stop believing that if you had only reported perfectly, none of this would have happened. There was likely no perfect way to report that would have protected you, because the conduct frame was available regardless, and the problem was never really your conduct.

Keep the original wrong in view

The single most important discipline in this chapter is to keep the original wrong in view, for yourself first, even as the institution works to bury it under your conduct. When the whole apparatus of the process is focused on your email, your tone, your professionalism, it becomes frighteningly easy to lose sight of what you actually reported, to start believing that the case really is about your behavior, to forget the wrong entirely under the weight of the redirection. Holding on to the original wrong, in your own mind and in your own records, is how you keep your bearings, because the moment you accept that the case is about your conduct, the reversal has fully succeeded.

This does not mean denying that your conduct was ever imperfect, which the next chapters address fully. It means refusing to let your imperfect conduct become the whole story, and keeping the thing you reported at the center of your own understanding even when the institution has moved it to the margins. Write down the original wrong. Keep the record of it. Return to it whenever the process tries to convince you that the real issue was your email. Caelis kept a single document at the top of his files, a plain statement of the staffing problem he had reported and the dates he had reported it, and he read it whenever the investigation into his conduct made him start to believe that he, and not the staffing crisis, was the problem, because that document was his hold on the truth the redirection was working to erase.

The shame that does the institution's work

The reversal's deepest hold in this chapter is not the institution's account but the shame you feel about your own conduct, because that shame makes you agree with the case against you. When you look back at your sharp email, your raised voice, your moment of visible anger, and feel a hot wave of shame, that shame quietly concludes that your conduct was the problem, that you were the one who behaved badly, that the institution is right to focus on you. The shame does the reversal's work from the inside, turning your own conscience into a witness against you, and as long as it runs unchallenged, no amount of understanding the redirection will fully free you.

Loosening the shame begins with placing your conduct accurately. A reaction to being ignored and mishandled for months is not the same as an act of unprovoked aggression, and feeling shame as though it were is a category error, however natural. This does not mean you approve of every word of the email, and the coming chapters give real room to own what is genuinely yours. But it means you stop treating your reaction as the whole story of your character or the true subject of the case, which is exactly what the institution needs you to do. Caelis learned to hold two truths at once: that he wished he had not sent that particular line, and that the line was the end of months of raising a real danger and did not make him the threat the hospital portrayed. The shame eased not when he excused the email but when he placed it correctly, as one moment inside a pattern that ran the other way.

When the process itself provokes you

There is a further cruelty worth naming, because it catches many people by surprise: the process the institution runs against you is frequently provoking, and your reactions to the process then become fresh evidence. Once you are the subject of an inquiry, you are subjected to delays, to accusations, to being treated as guilty, to having your character examined, and this treatment naturally produces frustration, anger, and distress. Those reactions to being mishandled by the process are then collected and added to the case, as though your entirely human response to being wrongly investigated were further proof that you are the difficult, unstable person the institution says you are. The process manufactures the very reactions it then cites.

Understanding this protects you from a trap that deepens as the process goes on. Every time the inquiry treats you unjustly and you react, you risk supplying more ammunition, and the institution can keep the cycle running indefinitely, provoking and then documenting, until the file is thick with your reactions and thin on the original wrong. The defense is not to feel nothing, which is impossible, but to know that the process is likely to provoke you and to route your reactions away from the process itself, into your records, your trusted people, and your professional support, so that your entirely legitimate anger does not become the next entry in the case against you. The later chapters build this discipline in full; for now it is enough to see that the process is not a neutral fact-finding but frequently a machine that produces the reactions it feeds on, and that your distress is the expected product of being wrongly investigated, not proof that the investigation was right.

What onlookers are shown

There is a final point worth making, because it explains why even fair-minded people at your institution may have come to see you as the problem. Colleagues, managers, and committee members who were not present for the months of your legitimate concern often have only your reaction to go on. They did not witness the staffing crisis, the stonewalling, the pattern of dismissal; they witnessed, or were shown, your sharp email, your frustrated outburst, the incident the institution chose to circulate. So even people with no wish to harm you can come away believing you were the difficult one, because the reaction is what reached them and the pattern never did.

Knowing this spares you a particular despair, the despair of concluding that because so many people seem to believe the worst, the worst must be true. The worst is simply what was shown. A person can be widely regarded within an institution as the difficult one and still have been the one who reported a real wrong and was reversed, because the thing that provoked their reaction stayed hidden while the reaction was put on display. This is not proof of your guilt; it is proof of what the institution chose to make visible, and the two are not the same.

Trying it on your own situation

Keep the wrong in view and place your reaction accurately.

First, write two separate statements: one naming the wrong you reported, and one naming whatever you did in reporting it that the institution has seized upon, your sharp email, your persistence, your emotional reaction. Keeping them on separate lines trains you to see the wrong and your reaction as two different things.

Second, place your reaction in its context. For whatever conduct the institution points to, write down what came before it: the months of being ignored, the dismissals, the specific event that finally produced your reaction. Placing the reaction back inside the pattern that produced it is the correction the redirection works to prevent.

Third, keep a single statement of the original wrong at the top of your records, with dates. Return to it whenever the process convinces you that your conduct was the real issue. That statement is your hold on what this was actually about.

Fourth, notice the shame when it comes, and name it. When you feel the hot wave about a sharp email or an angry moment, say to yourself: this was a reaction to being ignored and mishandled, not proof that I was the source of the problem. You are not excusing the reaction; you are placing it correctly, which is what the shame prevents. And when the process itself provokes a fresh reaction, route that reaction into your records and your trusted people rather than back into the process, so your legitimate anger does not become the next entry in the case against you.

What to carry forward

The institution converts your complaint, and your reaction to being mishandled, into the offense, shifting all attention to your tone, persistence, and conduct so the wrong you reported disappears. Your reaction is useful ammunition because a single sharp moment is vivid and documentable while the pattern of being dismissed that produced it is diffuse, and dramatic negative impressions form fast and stick (Baumeister et al., 2001), which means you cannot win by proving your reaction was justified. The language of professionalism and conduct is the institution's tool for this redirection, and it is a trap because the standard is applied selectively and the bar moves, so there was likely no perfect way to report that would have protected you. The single most important discipline is to keep the original wrong in view, for yourself and in your records, because the moment you accept that the case is about your conduct, the reversal has succeeded. Having learned to keep the wrong in view, the next chapter asks the hard question directly and gives you a fair way to answer it.

Chapter 3: Ask It Plainly: Did I Get This Wrong?

Vaelan lay awake for months turning over a question they could not put down: what if I was wrong. They were thirty-six, and they had reported a colleague for what they believed was serious financial misconduct, and the institution had cleared the colleague and turned its attention to Vaelan instead, suggesting the report had been reckless, motivated by a personal grievance, damaging to an innocent person. And in the dark, the institution's version began to seem possible. What if Vaelan had misread the evidence. What if the whole thing had been a terrible mistake, and Vaelan really was the one who had done harm, to a colleague who had done nothing. The fear was specific and cold: not that the institution was unfair, but that the institution was right, and that Vaelan was the reckless accuser the institution described. So this chapter met Vaelan where the fear lived, and asked the question plainly. Did I get this wrong. And working through it fairly, with a method rather than a slogan, did not confirm the fear. It resolved most of it, because the examination Vaelan had been dreading turned out to be the thing that finally let them stand on solid ground.

This chapter asks you to do the hardest and most freeing thing in the book: to ask, plainly and fairly, whether you got it wrong. I am not going to assure you that you were entirely right, because assurance you have not tested will not hold, and because a person of conscience deserves a real reckoning rather than a comforting slogan. Instead I am going to give you a structured way to examine your own conduct, one that can distinguish a genuine mistake or overreach, which you will own, from the false frame the institution has imposed, which you will refuse. This is the accountability spine of the book, and it runs in both directions: it protects a genuine reporter from a false charge, and it refuses to let anyone use these pages to dodge a real one.

Ask it plainly

The principle of this chapter is to ask the question plainly and answer it fairly. The reason to face it directly rather than avoid it is that the unasked question does not go away; it sits underneath everything, draining your confidence, because a fear you will not look at cannot be resolved. Asking whether you got it wrong, in good faith and with a method, is what lets you reach a grounded conclusion instead of oscillating forever between the institution's verdict and your own hope. And there is a point worth noticing at the outset: the very willingness to ask the question in earnest is itself a strong sign about you, because people who genuinely make reckless or malicious accusations are characteristically unwilling to examine themselves at all.

This willingness is the first thing to weigh. A person who truly reported in bad faith does not lie awake wondering whether they were wrong; they are untroubled, or they are focused on the damage they meant to do. The fact that you are asking the question at all, that you are prepared to consider that you might have erred, already distinguishes you from the reckless accuser the institution describes (Harsey, Zurbriggen, & Freyd, 2017). This does not settle the matter, and you should still do the examination. But notice, before you begin, that your fear of having gotten it wrong points in the opposite direction from where it feels like it points.

The five questions

The examination has five questions, and it works only if you answer them in writing and in good faith, prepared to find a genuine error if one is there. The first is the willingness question: are you genuinely willing to consider that you might have been mistaken or that you handled it badly. Hold that willingness, and notice equally any urge to convict yourself of everything, which is its own kind of avoidance. The second is the basis question: what did you actually report, and what was your basis for it. Write down the specific facts you had, the evidence you relied on, the reasonable grounds for your concern, setting aside the institution's later characterization of your motives.

The third question is the good-faith question: did you report in good faith, on reasonable grounds, believing the concern was real and worth raising. Reporting a genuine concern in good faith is not wrongdoing even if you turned out to be mistaken about some detail, and this question separates a good-faith report from a reckless or malicious one. The fourth is the conduct question: setting aside whether the concern was valid, was there something in how you handled it that you genuinely regret, a way you communicated, a step you skipped, a line you crossed. Answer this specifically, in terms of particular actions, not sweeping self-condemnation. And the fifth is the proportion question: looking at the whole, is the institution's response proportionate to any error you actually made, or wildly out of proportion, which is itself a strong sign of a reversal rather than a fair correction.

Two lists

Having worked through the five questions, you build two lists, and this is where the examination becomes usable. The first list is your genuine faults: the specific things you actually got wrong or handled badly, owned plainly, without inflation and without the character verdict. Many people who do this in good faith find some entries here, a detail they got wrong, a message they should have worded differently, a process step they skipped, and that is not a catastrophe. It is the ordinary texture of a real person handling a hard situation, and owning these is integrity, not defeat. The second list is the false frame: the institution's sweeping characterization of you as reckless, malicious, unstable, or the real problem, everything the institution piled onto you that the examination shows was not warranted. This list is what you refuse.

The discipline that makes this work is keeping the two lists strictly separate, because the reversal depends on fusing them, on making your genuine faults seem to prove the whole false frame. When Vaelan finally worked through the examination, they found a first list that was real but modest: they had overstated one figure in the report, and they had cc'd one person they should not have. And they found a second list that was large: the claim that the entire report had been reckless, that Vaelan was a malicious accuser, that they had set out to destroy an innocent colleague. The relief was not in having a blank first list, which almost no one has. It was in seeing, on paper, that the modest list of real faults did not add up to the large list of the false frame, and that owning the first did not require accepting the second (Neff, 2003).

The fair case for the other reading

Because this is the accountability chapter, it has to hold the other possibility open with equal seriousness, and not as a formality. It is possible that the examination will point, in part or even substantially, toward a real error on your part. Perhaps your basis was thinner than you told yourself. Perhaps you did report in a way that caused genuine and foreseeable harm to someone who did not deserve it. Perhaps some of what the institution says, stripped of its excess, contains something true that you have been avoiding. If that is what a fair examination shows, then the right response is not to reach for a more comfortable answer but to take up the accountability that a later chapter develops in full, which is how a person owns a real mistake without either denying it or collapsing into total self-condemnation.

This is what keeps the book from being a tool of evasion. A framework that only ever exonerated the reader would be worthless, because a genuinely reckless or malicious accuser could use it as easily as a wronged reporter, and you would have no way to tell which one you were. The value of the self-check is precisely that it can come out either way, which means that when it comes out in your favor, as it does for the great majority of people who have carried this so anxiously, the conclusion is worth something. You did not talk yourself into innocence; you tested the charge and it did not hold. And in the rarer case where it does hold in part, you have found something you can actually work with, which is far better than carrying an unexamined dread for the rest of your life.

It is worth saying what people usually find on the far side of this examination, because the dread beforehand is so heavy that many never cross to it. Almost everyone who works the five questions in good faith reports the same thing: the reckoning they feared would destroy them turns out to be the thing that steadies them. The fear whispered that a fair look would confirm the institution's verdict, and instead the fair look separated the real from the invented, gave the genuine errors a manageable size, and exposed the false frame as the thing it always was. What felt, in prospect, like walking toward a conviction turns out, in practice, to be walking out of a fog.

Why the institution's certainty is not evidence

One thing makes the self-check especially hard: the institution is so certain. It does not hedge; it states your fault through official channels, in the confident language of findings and conclusions, with the apparent weight of a process behind it. That institutional confidence can feel like proof that must outweigh your own tentative examination. It is worth seeing clearly why it is not. An institution defending itself needs the reporter to be at fault, because the alternative is facing its own wrongdoing and the cost of addressing it, which the whole apparatus is arranged to avoid. Its certainty is not the product of neutral weighing; it is the product of an interest, and an interest can generate confident findings while being completely wrong.

This is why you cannot resolve the question by deferring to the institution's conclusion. A process run by a body with a stake in the outcome is not the impartial tribunal it presents itself as, and its findings measure its interests as much as the facts. The formality is real, the letterhead is real, the procedure may even have been followed in form, and none of that makes the conclusion accurate, because a process can be procedurally tidy and substantively captured at the same time. Vaelan had taken the institution's finding as nearly final, reasoning that a whole official process could not simply be wrong. The self-check taught them a different lesson: that the process had been run by people whose institution was implicated, that its confident conclusion measured the institution's need to protect itself, and that the formality of the finding was not the same as its truth.

When you cannot be sure

Sometimes the examination does not deliver a clean verdict, and it would be untrue to pretend it always will. Evidence is incomplete, situations are complex, and a genuinely mixed case can leave you unsure exactly where the lines fall. If you finish the five questions and still cannot be certain, that uncertainty is not a failure of the method; it is an accurate result, and it is far better than a false certainty in either direction. You can hold a considered uncertainty, own the errors you are sure of, refuse the sweeping frame you are sure was not warranted, and leave the genuinely unclear middle as unclear, rather than forcing it to resolve in the institution's favor because that is the answer the process has been pressing on you.

What you should not do is treat uncertainty as a reason to default to the institution's verdict. The pull to do exactly that is strong, because the process is built to make its conclusion feel authoritative and your doubt feel like an admission. But a considered not sure is a legitimate resting place, and it is the ground on which you can keep living and keep observing, gathering understanding over time rather than settling the question prematurely against yourself. Vaelan found that a few aspects of the case stayed genuinely uncertain, and that they could carry that uncertainty without letting it collapse into the institution's story, holding what was clear on both lists while leaving the unclear open, to be understood better as more came to light.

Trying it on your own situation

Do the examination, in writing, in a calm hour.

First, work through the five questions on paper: willingness, basis, good faith, conduct, and proportion. Write real answers, not the answers you wish were true. The method only works if you are willing to find a genuine error where one is there.

Second, build your two lists. On the first, your genuine faults, specific and owned. On the second, the false frame, the sweeping characterization you refuse. Keep them visibly separate, because the whole discipline is in not letting the first list bleed into the second.

Third, write one sentence that states your grounded conclusion, drawn from the examination rather than from hope or fear. It might be: I made these specific errors, and I own them, and I reported a genuine concern in good faith and was not the reckless accuser the institution described. Reaching your own conclusion by method is what lets it hold when the institution's version comes at you again.

Fourth, if some aspects stayed genuinely unclear, list them separately under a heading of their own, and let them be unclear on purpose. Do not force the uncertain middle to resolve against yourself because the process has made its conclusion feel authoritative. Beside each unclear item, note one thing you could learn or observe over time that would help you understand it more accurately. Holding a considered uncertainty, rather than defaulting to the institution's verdict, is itself a refusal of the pressure the process puts on you to accept its account.

What to carry forward

Ask the question plainly, because the unasked fear drains you and only a fair examination can resolve it, and notice that your willingness to ask it already distinguishes you from the reckless accusers who never examine themselves (Harsey, Zurbriggen, & Freyd, 2017). Work the five questions, willingness, basis, good faith, conduct, and proportion, and build two lists: your genuine faults, which you own, and the false frame, which you refuse, keeping them strictly separate so the real does not seem to prove the false (Neff, 2003). A genuine concern reported in good faith on reasonable grounds is not wrongdoing even if some detail was mistaken, and a response wildly out of proportion to any real error is itself a sign of a reversal. Hold the other reading open with equal seriousness, because a check that only ever exonerated would be worthless, and if the examination points partly at your own conduct, the answer is real accountability rather than a more comfortable story. Having reached a grounded conclusion, the next chapter takes up how the institution rewrites reality, and why your own record is the ground you stand on.

Chapter 4: The Record Is Your Ground

Isoren started keeping records the day the story began to change, and it saved her sense of reality. She was thirty-nine, a university lecturer who had reported a senior colleague for a pattern of harassment, and the institution's response had been to tell her, again and again, that she had misunderstood. That was not what happened. No one else has raised any concern. You have taken this the wrong way. The policy does not mean what you think it means. Meeting by meeting, the events she had witnessed with her own eyes were revised in front of her, until she began to doubt what she had seen, to wonder whether she really had misread everything, to feel her grip on the facts loosening. And then, almost by accident, she found an old email that confirmed exactly what she remembered, and something steadied in her. The institution had spent months telling her that her memory was wrong, and here, in writing, was proof that it was not. From that day she wrote everything down, and the record became the ground she stood on when the institution tried to move it.

This chapter is about that experience, the institution's rewriting of reality, and about why your own record is the thing that keeps you standing. When an organization insists that events did not happen as you know they did, that you misunderstood, that no one else saw what you saw, it can wear down your confidence in your own perception until you no longer trust your account of your own experience. This is institutional gaslighting, and the answer to it is documentation: a record, kept in your own words and from the available evidence, that holds the facts steady when the institution works to dissolve them. Learning to keep that record, and to treat it as your ground, is one of the most practical and protective skills in the book.

The record is your ground

The principle of this chapter is that your record is the ground you stand on when the institution tries to move it. Against an organization's confident rewriting of what happened, your unaided memory is vulnerable, because memory is malleable and the institution's version is repeated with authority and in unison. A contemporaneous record, by contrast, is stable. Notes made at the time, emails saved, dates and details written down, these do not bend when the institution insists that things were otherwise, and they give you something outside your own contested memory to hold on to. The record is not primarily for winning an argument, though it may help with that. It is first for you, to keep your own grip on reality when the institution is working to loosen it.

This reframes documentation from a merely tactical activity into a protective one. You are not only building a file for a future dispute; you are building a bulwark against the disorientation the institution produces, a place where the facts are recorded and cannot be revised by the next meeting. When you begin to doubt whether you really saw what you saw, the record answers, in your own contemporaneous words, that you did. Isoren found that the practice of writing everything down did more than preserve evidence; it preserved her, because each entry was a small act of holding on to her own perception against an institution that was working, meeting by meeting, to take it from her.

Institutional gaslighting

It helps to understand what the institution is doing when it rewrites reality, because naming it as a recognized tactic loosens its hold. Gaslighting is the practice of undermining another person's confidence in their own perception of reality until they no longer trust their own mind, and it is not merely private cruelty; it draws on and exploits differences in power, which is exactly what an institution has in abundance (Sweet, 2019). When an organization tells you that what you plainly witnessed did not happen, that your interpretation is mistaken, that no one else shares your account, it is not simply disagreeing. It is using its authority, its numbers, and its control of the official record to dismantle your confidence in your own reality, which leaves you dependent on its version.

The institution is especially well equipped for this because it controls so much of what counts as the record. It writes the official minutes, issues the findings, holds the files, and speaks with the collective voice of many people and the weight of formal authority. Against all of that, your lone account can come to feel flimsy, and the sustained pressure of being told you are mistaken can produce exactly the self-doubt the institution needs. This is not evidence that you are actually unreliable; it is the designed effect of having your reality contested by a body with the power to make its version official. Isoren's growing uncertainty about what she had witnessed was not a sign that she had misperceived; it was the predictable result of institutional gaslighting, of having her account overwritten by an organization with every advantage in the contest over what was real.

Why you doubt yourself rather than them

There is a reason the doubt turns inward, against your own perception, rather than outward against the institution, and understanding it helps you resist the pull. You depended on this institution, and to see it clearly as the party distorting reality is threatening, because it means the body you relied on is acting against you, which is frightening and disorienting. It can feel safer, in a strange way, to conclude that you are the one who is mistaken, because that preserves the sense that the institution is basically trustworthy and the problem is just your own error. The mind reaches for the explanation that keeps the world intact, and doubting yourself keeps the institution intact in a way that seeing its betrayal does not.

This is the same protective logic that operates in betrayal by any depended-upon party: awareness bends away from the betrayer and toward the self, because facing the betrayal fully is harder than absorbing the blame (Freyd, 1996). Recognizing this lets you catch the reflex. When you find yourself concluding that you must be the one who is confused, you can ask whether that conclusion is the result of fair reflection or the pull to keep the institution trustworthy at the cost of your own perception. Often it is the latter, and the record is what lets you resist it, because the record does not care which conclusion is more comfortable; it simply holds what happened. Isoren learned to notice the moment she started to doubt herself and to reach for her file rather than for the reassuring conclusion that she had misunderstood, and the file told her, again and again, that she had not.

One caution keeps this practice from becoming its own trap. Keeping a record does not mean deciding that your memory is perfect or that you can never be mistaken about anything, which no person can truly claim. It means restoring your perception to the ordinary standing everyone else's enjoys: generally reliable, occasionally fallible, and yours to weigh rather than automatically surrendered to whoever contradicts it with the loudest authority. The record does not make you infallible; it makes you steady, which is what the institution's rewriting is designed to take from you. Steadiness, not certainty about every detail, is the goal, and the record is how you get it back.

How to keep the record

Keeping a useful record is a practical skill, and a few principles make it far more protective. Write things down as close to the time as possible, because contemporaneous notes are both more accurate and more credible than memory reconstructed later. Record specifics: dates, times, who was present, what was said, in plain factual language rather than interpretation. Preserve the documents you already have, emails, letters, messages, minutes, saved in a place the institution does not control, because material held only on a system the institution owns can vanish. And keep your record separate from your workplace or the institution's systems, in your own private space, so that it remains yours whatever happens to your access.

There is a companion practice worth adopting: writing your own account of significant events in your own words, promptly, before the institution's version has a chance to overwrite it. This is not about building a case so much as preserving your perception, giving your own account the status of a legitimate record rather than a suspect memory to be checked against the official one. Over time this private record becomes a store of stable reality that the institution's rewriting cannot reach, and returning to it is how you keep your bearings. A caution belongs here too: keep your documentation lawful and within your rights, and where recording or retaining certain material raises legal questions, that is one more reason to get proper advice. The point is not to gather ammunition by any means, but to preserve, lawfully and for yourself, a truthful record of what happened.

No one else has complained

One phrase deserves its own treatment, because institutions use it so reliably and it lands so hard: no one else has complained. It is offered as though it settled the matter, as though the absence of other complaints proved that nothing was wrong and that you are the outlier, the oversensitive one, the person imagining a problem no one else can see. It is worth understanding why this phrase is far weaker than it sounds. In an institution that punishes reporters, the absence of other complaints is exactly what you would expect, because the treatment you are receiving is precisely what deters everyone else from coming forward. People watch what happens to the person who reports, and they learn to stay silent, which means a low number of complaints can be a sign of an institution that suppresses them, not one where nothing is wrong.

Seeing this frees you from a particular trap. When the institution tells you that no one else has complained, the implication is that you are uniquely mistaken, and the natural response is to doubt yourself: if it were real, surely others would have said something. But others may well have witnessed the same thing and chosen, reasonably, to protect themselves by staying quiet, especially once they saw the reversal aimed at you. The silence of others is not evidence that you are wrong; it is often evidence that they are afraid, and their fear is a rational response to exactly the treatment you are now experiencing. Isoren later learned that two other colleagues had witnessed the harassment she reported and had said nothing precisely because they had seen what happened to her, which turned the institution's no one else has complained from proof of her error into proof of its own chilling effect.

When the doubt goes deep

For some people the institutional gaslighting reaches beyond particular events into a more general erosion, a growing sense that they cannot trust their own judgment about anything, that maybe they really are the unreliable person the institution describes. If months of being told you misperceive, misunderstand, and overreact have left you doubting your basic grip on reality, that is a heavy burden, and it is worth naming directly and answering directly. The experience of doubting your own perception, when that perception has been systematically undermined by a body with power over you, is not a sign that something is wrong with your mind. It is the expected effect of the undermining, a wound rather than a defect.

It is also a reason to protect and rebuild your confidence deliberately, and sometimes with help. The record is the first tool, and for many people it is enough to restore their footing. But if the doubt has gone deep, if you find yourself unable to trust your perception even where the record confirms it, that is a good reason to work with a skilled professional, not because you are as unreliable as the institution claimed, but because rebuilding trust in your own mind after it has been deliberately eroded is often more than a person can do without support. Seeking that help is not a concession that the institution was right about you; it is a way of undoing the specific injury the institution inflicted, which was to make you doubt a mind that was working correctly all along.

Trying it on your own situation

Build the record that will be your ground.

First, start writing things down now, as close to the time as you can. For each significant event, record the date, who was present, and what was said or done, in plain factual language. Contemporaneous notes are both more accurate and more stabilizing than memory recalled later.

Second, preserve the documents you already have and keep your record in your own private space, not on a system the institution controls. Material held only where the institution can reach it can disappear; material you hold is yours.

Third, when you feel your grip on reality loosening, when you start to believe you must have misunderstood, reach for the record rather than for the reassuring conclusion that you were wrong. Let the contemporaneous facts, in your own words, answer the doubt the institution has planted.

Fourth, when the institution tells you that no one else has complained, do not accept it as proof that you are mistaken. Write down, for yourself, the alternative reading: in a place that punishes reporters, the silence of others is often fear, not evidence that nothing is wrong. And if the doubt has gone deep enough that you cannot trust your perception even where the record confirms it, treat that as a reason to seek a skilled professional, not as a verdict on your mind. Rebuilding trust in a mind that was deliberately undermined is real recovery work, and needing help with it is a sign you are taking your own restoration seriously.

What to carry forward

Your record is the ground you stand on when the institution tries to move it, because against an organization's confident rewriting your unaided memory is vulnerable while a contemporaneous record is stable, and the record is first for you, to keep your grip on reality. Institutional gaslighting undermines your confidence in your own perception by exploiting the institution's authority, numbers, and control of the official record (Sweet, 2019), so your growing self-doubt is the designed effect of the tactic, not evidence that you are unreliable. The doubt turns inward because seeing the institution you depended on as the distorter is threatening, so awareness bends toward self-blame to keep the institution trustworthy (Freyd, 1996), and catching that reflex is how you resist it. Keep the record contemporaneously, specifically, lawfully, and in your own private space, and write your own account of events promptly, so you have a store of stable reality the institution's rewriting cannot reach. With your footing secured by the record, the next chapter teaches you to read the institution by power and direction rather than by its polished procedures.

Chapter 5: Follow the Power, Not the Politeness

Évren was reassured by the process right up until the moment it destroyed him. He was forty-seven, a civil servant who had reported procurement irregularities, and from the beginning the institution had been impeccably polite. There were meetings, and acknowledgments, and an independent-sounding review, and people who spoke warmly of taking his concerns seriously and following due process. Évren, who believed in process, found this reassuring, and he cooperated fully, trusting that the machinery of fairness was grinding toward a fair result. It was only near the end, when the review cleared everyone he had reported and quietly recommended that his own position be reconsidered, that he understood what he had been watching. The politeness had never been fairness. The process had been designed to arrive at a predetermined destination, and its courtesy had been the anesthetic that kept him cooperative while it worked. He had been reading the institution by its manners, when he should have been reading it by its power.

This chapter gives you the lens Évren found too late: a way to read an institution not by its language, its procedures, and its professed values, but by the direction its power actually runs. Institutions are skilled at the appearance of fairness, at courteous meetings and neutral-sounding processes that feel like justice while delivering the opposite. If you have been reassured by an institution's politeness, or confused because the process looked fair but the outcome was fixed, this chapter offers a more accurate reading. The question is not whether the institution is being civil or following procedure. The question is which way its power runs, whom it is protecting, and where the process is actually heading, because that direction, not the courtesy, is what tells you what is happening to you.

Follow the power, not the politeness

The principle of this chapter is to read the institution by the direction of its power, not by its politeness. An institution's civility, its neutral language, its formal procedures, these tell you almost nothing about whether you are being treated fairly, because an institution can be scrupulously polite and procedurally correct while protecting the wrongdoer and sacrificing you. Fairness is not a matter of tone or form; it is a matter of where the power runs and whom the outcome serves. To read your situation accurately, you stop asking whether the institution is being courteous and start asking whom its power is protecting, because the answer to that question, not the quality of the manners, is what reveals the reality.

This lens dissolves the confusion that politeness creates. A process can have every appearance of fairness, independent reviewers, careful meetings, respectful language, and still be structured to reach a conclusion that protects the institution and blames you. The courtesy is not evidence of fairness; it is often the mechanism by which an unfair process keeps you cooperative and makes its eventual conclusion look legitimate. When you read by the direction of power instead, you ask the questions that actually locate you: who benefits from the likely outcome, who is being protected, whose interests the process serves. Évren had been reading the warmth of the meetings as a sign of good faith, when the only reliable sign was the direction the power ran, which was, from the start, toward protecting the institution and away from him.

Reading the direction of power

To read the direction of power in your own situation, you ask a set of concrete questions that cut through the appearance of fairness. Whom does the likely outcome protect: the institution and the people it cannot afford to lose, or the person who reported. Who controls the process: an independent body with real power to hold the institution accountable, or people whose careers and loyalties are bound up with the institution itself. Where do the incentives run: does anyone with power over the outcome have an interest in finding against the institution, or does everyone with power benefit from finding against you. These questions reveal the direction of the power, and the direction of the power predicts the outcome far better than the politeness of the process does.

Applying these questions is often clarifying and sometimes stark. In many institutional situations, the people running the process all share an interest in protecting the institution, the reviewers are not truly independent, and the incentives all run one way, toward finding that the reporter, not the institution, was the problem. This does not mean every process is rigged, and some institutions do act with integrity. But reading the direction of power tells you which kind of process you are in, and it tells you not to mistake courtesy for fairness. Évren realized, once he asked whom the review protected and who controlled it, that the answer had been visible all along: the reviewers reported to the very leadership implicated in the procurement, and every incentive ran toward clearing them, which the politeness had disguised but never changed.

Pattern over incident, direction over process

Just as individuals hide a pattern behind isolated incidents, institutions hide the direction of their power behind the procedural steps of a process. If you focus on each step of the process in isolation, whether this meeting was conducted properly, whether that letter was worded fairly, you can be kept busy indefinitely evaluating the fairness of individual steps while the overall direction, the destination the whole process is heading toward, escapes your notice. A process can be composed of individually unobjectionable steps and still be aimed, as a whole, at a predetermined and unjust conclusion. The direction of the whole is what matters, and it is precisely what attention to individual steps obscures.

This is why the abuse-reading question that runs through these books, direction and power over time rather than isolated incidents, applies to institutions as much as to individuals (Stark, 2007). You read the institution not by whether each procedural step was polite and correct, but by the sustained direction of its power across the whole matter: consistently protecting the same interests, consistently disadvantaging the same person, consistently arriving at conclusions that serve the institution. That sustained direction is the pattern, and it is far more revealing than any single step. Évren had evaluated each meeting on its own and found each one reasonable, which was exactly how he had missed the direction of the whole, a process that had been heading toward his removal from the first day, one courteous step at a time.

The betrayal of believing in the institution

There is a particular grief for people like Évren, who believed in the institution and its processes, and it is worth naming because it is part of what has to be worked through. If you were someone who trusted in fair process, who believed that institutions, whatever their flaws, ultimately tried to do right, then discovering that the process was a mechanism rather than a search for truth is not only a practical defeat but the loss of a belief you lived by. The disillusionment can be profound, because you are losing not just this case but a faith in institutions that shaped how you understood the world. That grief is real, and it deserves acknowledgment rather than being rushed past.

It is worth holding this grief without letting it curdle into a cynicism that says every institution is corrupt and no process can be trusted, which is as inaccurate as the naive faith it replaces. The truth is more useful and more bearable: institutions are systems with interests, capable of both integrity and betrayal, and they must be read by the direction of their power rather than trusted or distrusted wholesale. Learning to read them this way is not cynicism; it is accuracy, and it is a more durable footing than either blind faith or blanket suspicion.

Évren came, over time, to a clearer and sadder wisdom than the faith he had lost: not that institutions are always corrupt, but that they must be watched by where their power runs, and never trusted merely because they are polite.

Why the appearance of fairness is so disarming

It is worth dwelling on why an institution's polished process disarms people so thoroughly, because understanding the mechanism is what breaks its hold. The appearance of fairness works on decent people precisely because they are decent. A person who believes in fairness extends good faith, assumes that a courteous process is a fair one, and cooperates fully, giving the institution their candor and their patience, because that is what a fair process would deserve. The institution then draws on exactly that good faith, using the reporter's willingness to trust the process as the means of keeping them cooperative and unguarded while the process moves toward its predetermined end. The better a person you are, the more the appearance of fairness can be used against you, which is a bitter thing to learn.

Seeing this protects you from a particular self-reproach, the feeling that you were foolish to trust the process, that you should have seen through it sooner. You trusted the process because trusting fair processes is reasonable and decent, and the institution engineered the appearance of fairness precisely to earn that trust. The failure was not in your good faith but in an institution that exploited it. This does not mean you should now trust nothing, but it does mean you read the process by its direction rather than its manners, and you keep your own counsel and your own records even inside a process that feels fair, because feeling fair is exactly what a captured process is designed to do. Évren stopped blaming himself for having cooperated once he understood that his cooperation had been the reasonable response of a person who believed in fairness, and that the institution had counted on exactly that belief.

Reading direction does not mean refusing to participate

A clarification matters here, because reading the direction of an institution's power can tip people into a despair that says the outcome is fixed, so there is no point in participating at all. That is not the lesson. Reading the direction of power is not a reason to disengage; it is a reason to participate with clear eyes rather than false comfort. You may have very good reasons to take part in a process even when you can see its likely direction: to build a record, to preserve later options, to meet legal or procedural requirements, to give an institution that might yet act with integrity the chance to do so. What changes is not whether you participate but how: you participate without mistaking courtesy for safety, without surrendering your records or your bearings, and without staking your wellbeing on a fair outcome you have reason to doubt.

This is the difference between naive participation and clear-eyed participation. The naive participant trusts the process, relaxes their guard, and is undone when the direction reveals itself. The clear-eyed participant engages fully with the process while reading its direction, keeping their own record, seeking their own advice, and holding their sense of themselves apart from the institution's likely verdict. Reading the direction of power does not tell you to walk away; it tells you to walk in awake. Évren often wished he had not disengaged emotionally from his own life while trusting the process, but he did not conclude that he should have refused to participate; he concluded that he should have participated while watching where the power ran, which would have let him protect himself without either false hope or premature surrender.

The independent review that is not

One institutional device deserves a specific warning, because it fools so many people: the independent review. When an institution announces that it has commissioned an independent investigation, an outside firm, an external panel, a neutral reviewer, the word independent does a great deal of reassuring work, and it is often unearned. A review is only as independent as its terms, its reporting lines, and its incentives allow, and an institution that is paying for a review, setting its scope, choosing its questions, and receiving its findings retains enormous influence over what that review can conclude. The label independent describes who conducts the review, not who controls it, and those are frequently not the same.

To read such a review by the direction of power, ask the concrete questions rather than accepting the label. Who chose the reviewer and who pays them. Who set the scope of what would be examined and what would be left out. To whom does the reviewer report, and who decides what happens to the findings. If the answers all run back to the institution and its leadership, the review is independent in name and captured in substance, however distinguished the reviewer. This does not mean every external review is a sham, but it means you weigh it by its structure and incentives, not by the reassuring word attached to it. Évren had taken the independence of his review on trust, and learned too late that its scope had been drawn to exclude precisely the leadership it should have examined.

Trying it on your own situation

Read your institution by the direction of its power.

First, ask the direction-of-power questions in writing. Whom does the likely outcome protect. Who controls the process, and are they truly independent of the institution. Where do the incentives of the people with power over the outcome actually run. The answers reveal the direction that the politeness disguises.

Second, take the reassurance you have drawn from the institution's courtesy or its procedures, and test it against the direction of power. Ask not whether the process has been civil and correct in its steps, but where the whole process is heading and whom it serves.

Courtesy is not fairness, and correct steps can compose an unjust whole.

Third, if you trusted in fair process and are losing that faith, let yourself grieve the loss without swinging to the belief that all institutions are corrupt. The accurate position is that institutions must be read by the direction of their power, which is a steadier footing than either faith or blanket suspicion.

Fourth, decide how you will participate now that you can read the direction. Reading the power is not a reason to disengage but a reason to engage with clear eyes: to keep your own records, seek your own advice, meet the requirements that preserve your later options, and hold your sense of yourself apart from the institution's likely verdict. Write down, for your own situation, what participating awake looks like, so that you neither relax into a false trust nor surrender before you have to.

What to carry forward

Read the institution by the direction of its power, not by its politeness, because an organization can be scrupulously civil and procedurally correct while protecting the wrongdoer and sacrificing you, and fairness is a matter of where the power runs and whom the outcome serves rather than of tone or form. Ask whom the likely outcome protects, who controls the process, and where the incentives run, because those answers reveal the direction the courtesy disguises. Read the direction of the whole rather than the fairness of individual steps, because a process of individually unobjectionable steps can be aimed as a whole at a predetermined and unjust conclusion, and direction and power over time is the accurate reading for institutions as for individuals (Stark, 2007). If you believed in fair process, grieve the loss of that faith without swinging to blanket cynicism, because the accurate and more durable position is to read institutions by the direction of their power. Having learned to read the institution accurately, the next chapter prepares you for what happens when colleagues and committees close ranks against you.

Chapter 6: When Everyone Closes Ranks

Solenne watched her colleagues go quiet one by one, and the silence was worse than any attack. She was forty-two, a researcher who had reported a senior figure for taking credit for junior colleagues' work and worse, and in the early days several colleagues had told her privately that they knew she was right, that they had seen it too, that they supported her. Then the institution began its response, and the private support did not become public. The colleagues who had agreed with her in the corridor stopped meeting her eye. The ones who had said they would speak up did not. Committees she had served on for years reached conclusions that treated her as the problem. And Solenne experienced something she had not been prepared for: not the hostility of enemies, which she could have borne, but the withdrawal of people she had trusted, the slow closing of ranks by an entire professional community that had, only weeks before, seemed to be on her side. She had expected the institution to defend itself. She had not expected everyone else to let it.

This chapter is about that closing of ranks, and about the particular desolation of watching a whole professional community side with the institution or fall silent. Facing the institution itself is painful; facing the withdrawal of colleagues, the silence of people who know you are right, the committees that reach against you, is one of the most isolating experiences a working life can hold. This chapter explains why people close ranks around an institution, why even those who privately agree with you go quiet, and how to stay steady when the community you belonged to has, in effect, decided you are the problem. Understanding the closing of ranks is what keeps you from taking it as proof that you were wrong.

Steady when the community turns

The principle of this chapter is to stay steady when the community turns, rather than trying to win it back. When colleagues fall silent and committees close ranks, the natural impulse is to reach each person, to remind them of what they said privately, to rally the support you thought you had, because the injustice of being abandoned by people who know better is unbearable. This impulse is understandable and it is largely a trap: the campaign to rally your colleagues is exhausting, usually unsuccessful, and prone to making you look like the embattled, difficult person the institution says you are. Staying steady means declining that campaign and holding your ground without needing the community's public support.

This is hard, because the silence of colleagues feels like a verdict, and reaching them feels like the only way to overturn it. But you cannot argue a whole community into risking themselves for you, and the effort to do so drains you while confirming the institution's picture of you as the person consumed by a grievance. The steadiness this chapter teaches is not resignation; it is the deliberate choice to stop spending your energy on a community that has, for its own reasons, decided not to stand with you publicly, and to keep that energy instead for your own clarity, your recovery, and the few who will actually stand with you. You do not restore your standing by winning the community back. You restore yourself by ceasing to require its public verdict in order to know who you are.

Why colleagues who agree with you go silent

To stop taking your colleagues' silence as proof of your guilt, you have to understand why they go quiet, because their silence is not the judgment on you that it feels like. Most colleagues who fall silent are not concluding that you were wrong; they are protecting themselves. They have watched the reversal aimed at you, seen what happens to the person who crosses the institution, and drawn the entirely rational conclusion that speaking up would put them in your position. Their silence is a measure of the institution's power to punish, not a measure of your rightness, and the fact that they agreed with you privately and abandoned you publicly tells you exactly that: they know you are right, and they are afraid.

This reframing matters because the silence of people who know the truth is one of the most disorienting parts of the whole experience, and it is easy to read it as evidence that you must be wrong after all, since no one will stand with you. But people can know you are right and still refuse to stand with you, because standing with you is dangerous, and self-protection is a powerful motive. Their fear is real, and it is often justified, given what they have watched happen to you. Solenne came to understand that her colleagues' silence was not a statement that she was mistaken; it was a statement about what the institution did to people who spoke, and their withdrawal, painful as it was, confirmed rather than denied the reality of what she had reported.

Why observers come to believe the institution

Beyond those who privately agree and stay silent, there are colleagues and observers who genuinely come to believe the institution's version, and understanding how that happens protects you from taking their belief as proof. When people are exposed to the reversal, the deny, attack, and reverse pattern, their judgment tends to shift toward the party using the tactic and against the target: the reporter comes to seem less credible and the institution more so, simply as an effect of the tactic being deployed (Harsey & Freyd, 2020). So the colleagues who come to see you as the problem are not necessarily weighing the evidence and finding you guilty; they are being moved by the reversal itself, which is designed to produce exactly that shift in observers.

This is reinforced by how institutions manage the story. The institution speaks with calm authority and a single coordinated voice, while you, the individual, respond with the natural intensity of someone being wronged, and calm authority reads as credibility while intensity reads as instability, regardless of who is telling the truth. Add that negative, dramatic impressions of you spread quickly and stick, while the diffuse truth of your original report does not travel nearly as well (Baumeister et al., 2001), and you have a situation in which observers drift toward the institution's version through no fair weighing at all. Solenne watched colleagues who had no stake in harming her nonetheless come to speak of her as difficult, and understood that they were not concluding she was wrong so much as being carried by a reversal built to carry them.

The distinct wound of professional abandonment

It is worth naming directly that being abandoned by your professional community is a distinct and severe wound, layered on top of the original betrayal, and its pain is real and recognized. There is a particular desolation in losing the colleagues, the standing, the belonging of a working life, in watching a community you contributed to for years treat you as an outsider or a problem. This is not the same as a stranger's hostility; it reaches something deeper, because your professional community was part of your identity and your security, and to be cast out of it touches both your livelihood and your sense of who you are. When an institution and a community you depended on turn away, that betrayal becomes a second injury, distinct from and often more damaging than the original wrong (Smith & Freyd, 2014).

Naming this wound matters because you may be underestimating it, treating your devastation as an overreaction when it is a proportionate response to a real and serious loss. The grief of professional abandonment, of losing the belonging and standing of a working life, deserves to be taken seriously rather than minimized as mere workplace trouble. It is a genuine bereavement, and treating it as one, rather than scolding yourself for feeling it so deeply, is part of an accurate response to what has actually happened to you.

Solenne had to learn to grieve the loss of her professional world as the real loss it was, rather than telling herself it was only a job and only colleagues, because minimizing the loss did not lessen it; it only left her mourning something she would not let herself name.

Why correcting the community backfires

The impulse to reach each colleague and set the record straight deserves closer attention, because it is so strong and understanding why it fails is what lets you set it down. When people you trusted fall silent or drift toward the institution's version, every instinct wants to reach them, to remind them of what they saw, to show them the evidence, to recover the support you thought you had. Yet the campaign backfires with grim reliability, for reasons worth seeing plainly. To a colleague who has heard the institution's calm account and now receives your intense, detailed appeal, the very intensity reads as instability, and the effort to rally them reads as the conduct of a person consumed by grievance, which is precisely the picture the institution has painted. Your reasonable attempt to recover your community becomes further evidence for the story that you are the problem.

Seeing this lets you stop fighting on ground where you are set up to lose. The reversal has arranged things so that your human need to be believed by your colleagues becomes, when you act on it, more proof of the institution's case. The way through is not to appeal harder or more calmly, though calm helps, but largely to decline the campaign and let your steady conduct over time speak where your appeals cannot. Solenne's early attempts to remind colleagues of what they had told her privately only made her seem, to people half-watching, like someone who could not let go, and it was when she stopped, when she let the matter rest and simply carried herself steadily, that a few of those colleagues, in their own time, began quietly to acknowledge what they knew.

The community corrects itself slowly, or it does not

There is a longer truth about the community worth holding, because it offers a realistic hope in place of a false one. Some colleagues, over time, do come to stand with you, or at least to acknowledge the truth privately, not because you argued them into it but because your steady conduct across the months accumulates against a story that needs constant retelling to survive. A false account of you has to be maintained; your actual character only has to be lived. As you go on being, visibly and consistently, a person whose conduct does not match the institution's portrait, a gap opens between the portrait and the reality, and some observers notice the gap on their own, which is worth more than any correction you could have pressed on them.

But it would be a false promise to say the whole community will come around, because some will not, and building your recovery on the hope that they eventually will keeps you tethered to their verdict. The realistic position is to do the one thing in your power, to live steadily as yourself, and to release the outcome, accepting that some colleagues will drift back toward you, some will not, and none of it is within your control. This is neither optimism nor despair; it is accuracy, and accuracy is more livable than either. Solenne came to hold her professional community loosely, tending the few who stood with her and her life outside the institution, and found over several years that some colleagues quietly returned while others never did, and that she could live well without waiting to learn which would be which.

Steadiness, in the end, is the whole answer to the closing of ranks, and it is worth being clear about what steadiness is not. It is not indifference, and it does not require you to stop caring that a community you gave years to has turned away, which would be neither possible nor healthy. It is the practiced choice to keep living and working as yourself while the community does what it does, refusing to let its silence set the terms of your days. The closing of ranks is loud in its way, even when it is silent, and steadiness is quiet, and quiet outlasts the pressure, because the institution's story needs constant maintenance while your life only needs to be lived.

Trying it on your own situation

Stay steady when the community turns, and steady yourself instead.

First, sort the people in your professional world into three groups: those who might actually stand with you, those who are firmly aligned with the institution, and those who are silent out of fear. Deciding where your limited energy goes, and where it does not, is the beginning of steadiness. The firmly aligned are not your audience, and the silent are not your judges.

Second, when a colleague's silence feels like a verdict, name it accurately: their silence is usually fear of what the institution does to people who speak, not a judgment that I was wrong. Their withdrawal often confirms the reality of what you reported rather than denying it.

Third, let yourself grieve the wound of professional abandonment as the real loss it is, rather than minimizing it as mere workplace trouble. Name the loss of your community and standing as a genuine bereavement, so you can mourn it fully instead of treating your own devastation as an overreaction.

Fourth, choose one thing you will stop doing this month in the campaign to win back your colleagues: the reminders of what they said privately, the forwarding of evidence, the appeals to people who have already chosen safety. Notice that stopping is not conceding the institution's story; it is declining a contest where your visible distress becomes further proof against you. Write down what you will do instead with that time and energy, whether tending the few who stand with you or simply living steadily, because steady conduct over time reaches observers in a way no appeal can.

What to carry forward

Stay steady when the community turns, rather than trying to win it back, because you cannot argue a whole community into risking themselves for you, and the campaign to rally them exhausts you while confirming the institution's picture of you. Colleagues who privately agree and then go silent are usually protecting themselves, not judging you, so their silence measures the institution's power to punish and often confirms the reality of what you reported. Observers who come to believe the institution are frequently moved by the reversal itself, which shifts credibility toward the tactic-user and against the target (Harsey & Freyd, 2020), and by the institution's calm coordinated voice against your natural intensity, with negative impressions of you spreading fast and sticking (Baumeister et al., 2001). Professional abandonment is a distinct and severe wound, a betrayal by a community you depended on (Smith & Freyd, 2014), and it deserves to be grieved as the real loss it is. Having learned to stand steady against the closing of ranks, the next chapter gives you a way to respond when the institution comes at you through its process.

Chapter 7: Answer the Process, Not the Shame

Auren used to write ten-page responses to every letter the institution sent him, and every one of them was used against him. He was forty-five, an academic under investigation after reporting a colleague's research misconduct, and each time the institution sent him an accusation or a request for his account, he would sit up half the night composing an exhaustive reply: the full history, the corrections of every distortion, the evidence, the context, his feelings about the injustice of it all. He believed that if he just explained thoroughly enough, the truth would become undeniable. Instead, his long responses gave the investigation more material to mine, more sentences to quote out of context, more evidence of his emotional investment, more surface to attack. The exchanges grew, the file thickened, and Auren exhausted himself producing the very ammunition being turned against him. What changed his situation was not a better ten-page response. It was learning to answer the process narrowly, in writing, on the record, and to keep everything he actually felt somewhere the process could not reach.

This chapter is about how to respond when the institution comes at you through its process: the accusatory letter, the request for your account, the meeting, the investigation. Most people in your position respond in one of two losing ways: they over-explain, pouring out exhaustive defenses that give the process endless material, or they freeze, unable to respond at all. This chapter offers a third way, a narrow, calm, documented response that answers what genuinely needs answering and declines the rest, and that keeps the enormous emotional pressure of the process routed somewhere it can do no harm. Answering the process and not the shame is how you stop feeding the machine that has been consuming you.

Answer the process, not the shame

The principle of this chapter is to answer the process and not the shame. An institutional communication usually contains two things: specific, answerable points that may genuinely require a response, and a much larger attack on your character, credibility, and worth. The mistake is to respond to the whole thing, to defend your character against the attack, when the attack is not a question to be answered but a hook to be declined. Answering the process means addressing the specific, answerable points factually and on the record, and refusing to engage the character attack, because the character attack is the shame the process is trying to activate, and every attempt to answer it feeds it.

This distinction is the whole discipline. When the institution characterizes you as reckless, difficult, or untrustworthy, there is almost nothing there to answer, because it is not a factual question but a bid to make you defend your whole self. When it asks a specific question, what did you do on a particular date, what is your account of a particular event, that is answerable, and you answer it factually and briefly, on the record. What you do not do is write the ten-page defense of your character, because your character is not a question any response can resolve; it is being attacked in order to pull you into producing more material. Answering the process and not the shame keeps your response narrow, factual, documented, and hard to use against you, which is exactly what the reversal cannot easily exploit.

Everything in writing, on the record

For institutional situations specifically, one discipline matters more than almost any other: keep the important exchanges in writing and on the record. Where you can, and where it is lawful and appropriate, conduct significant communications in writing rather than in conversations that leave no trace, because a written record protects you against the later rewriting of what was said. When you are required to attend meetings, follow up afterward in writing with your own account of what was discussed and agreed, so that there is a record in your words and not only in theirs. The institution controls the official record; your contemporaneous written communications are part of how you keep a truthful account that it does not fully control.

This is not about being adversarial for its own sake; it is about protecting yourself in a situation where the spoken word can be denied and the official record can be shaped. A calm, factual, written response to an accusation both answers what needs answering and creates a record of your having answered it reasonably, which serves you far better than an unrecorded conversation in which your words can later be characterized however the institution wishes. There is a caution here too: written records can be disclosed in formal proceedings, so what you write should be measured, factual, and something you would be content to have read by an impartial outside reader, which is exactly the discipline the next section describes. Auren learned to move as much as he could into writing, and to keep his written responses calm and narrow, because he came to understand that in an institutional fight, the unrecorded word was dangerous and the measured written word was protection.

The third reader

A single practice makes the narrow written response far easier to produce well, and it runs through these books: write everything you send as though a fair, impartial outside reader will one day read it. Before you send any response to the institution, imagine that a neutral third party, a reasonable person with no stake in the matter, will read it later, and write it so that this reader would see a calm, factual, reasonable person. This third reader is a device for keeping your communications measured, because it naturally strips out the heat, the counter-attacks, the pleading, and the character defense, leaving the factual, on-the-record response that serves you.

The third reader also protects you from the reversal's favorite trap, which is to provoke you into a response that looks bad out of context. When you write for the third reader, you do not send the furious paragraph, the sarcastic line, the desperate over-explanation, because you can see how each would look to a neutral observer, and so the process gains no vivid moment to quote against you. This is not about suppressing your feelings, which have somewhere else to go, but about ensuring that what you commit to the record is only ever what a fair reader would find reasonable. Auren began running every response past the imagined third reader before sending it, and found that the practice did in seconds what his agonized editing had never managed: it produced responses that were brief, factual, and impossible to make him look bad with, because a reasonable reader would have found nothing in them but a reasonable person.

Handle the pressure somewhere else

The narrow response only works if you have somewhere to put the enormous emotional pressure that an institutional process creates, because that pressure is real and it has to go somewhere. If you swallow it entirely and let it build, it will eventually burst out, often in exactly the flood or fury the reversal is fishing for. So the discipline of the measured response is not about suppressing what you feel; it is about routing that feeling away from the record and toward a place where it can be safely discharged. You write the furious ten-page reply, and you do not send it; you say what you feel to a trusted friend, a therapist, an advocate, or a private page, where it harms no one and gives the process nothing.

This is why the people who manage the narrow response are not the ones with superhuman composure but the ones with somewhere to take their distress. The rage at the injustice, the grief of the betrayal, the longing to finally be believed, all of it is valid and all of it needs expression, just not in the response to the institution or on the record. When you have a genuine outlet for the feeling, the measured response stops feeling like suppression and starts feeling like strategy, because the feeling is fully honored, just in a place where it can do some good instead of becoming the next entry in your file. Auren found that once he poured his real reactions into a journal and a trusted friend rather than into his responses, the narrow written reply stopped costing him so much, because the feeling had a home and the record did not have to carry it.

Why the long defense makes it worse

It is worth understanding precisely why the exhaustive reply backfires, because the urge to send it is so strong that only seeing the mechanism will loosen it. When you pour out a full defense, you are trying to be believed, to make the institution finally see the truth of your position, and that longing is entirely human. But a full defense hands the process two things it needs. It gives the investigators a wealth of material to comb, quote out of context, and turn into fresh lines of inquiry, because a long document contains many sentences that can be lifted and reframed. And it displays your emotional investment, showing exactly which points are live and which accusations land, which is precisely the map a process running the reversal uses to aim its next move.

Seeing this changes the calculation. The long reply feels like your best chance to be believed, and it is in fact your greatest exposure, because everything you reveal in the attempt to be believed becomes a tool for a process that has no intention of believing you. The narrow response protects you not by hiding the truth but by declining to hand it to a process that will only misuse it. Auren's exhaustive replies had been, without his knowing it, a gift to the investigation, a detailed inventory of his feelings, his history, and his vulnerabilities that could be drawn on indefinitely. When he stopped supplying the inventory and answered only what genuinely required an answer, the process had far less to work with, because you cannot reframe a paragraph that was never written.

Dignity in the narrow response

There is a further point worth making, because the narrow response can feel, at first, like a surrender, like letting the accusation stand unanswered. It is the opposite. Refusing to perform the role the process assigns you, declining to rage or grovel or flood the file, keeping your responses measured and your feeling in its proper place, is the most dignified course available to you inside an institutional reversal. Dignity, unlike frantic defense, is legible over time to anyone who later reviews the record, and it is legible to you, which matters most, because each measured response is a small act of self-respect that tells you, in your own conduct, that you are not the person the institution describes.

This is why the narrow response is not only strategic but restorative. Every time you decline to be provoked into a damaging reply, you demonstrate to yourself that you can receive an accusation and choose your response, which is direct evidence against the institution's picture of you as the volatile, difficult one. You do not restore your standing by winning the argument inside a captured process, which usually cannot be won on the institution's terms; you restore it by being, steadily and unmistakably, a person whose conduct on the record does not match the story, until the gap between the two is the most visible thing in the file. Auren came to see his brief, measured responses not as surrenders but as the clearest statement he could make of who he actually was, made not in words of self-defense but in the simple fact of his composure on the record.

Underneath the long defenses lies a single wish worth naming, because it is the engine of the whole losing pattern: the wish to finally be believed by the institution. You do not write the exhaustive reply to win a procedural point; you write it because some part of you still believes that if you could just explain it well enough, the institution would see, and the whole reversal would dissolve. That wish is human, and it is exactly what keeps you feeding the process, because it treats the institution as an audience that could be reached, when the reversal is built precisely to prevent it from reaching you. The next chapter takes up that wish directly, because releasing it is the hardest and most freeing move left.

Trying it on your own situation

Practice the narrow, documented response.

First, take a recent institutional communication and separate it into two parts: the specific, answerable points, and the character attack or credibility bid. Draft a brief, factual, on-the-record reply to the specific points, and plan to decline the rest entirely. Seeing the two parts separately is what makes the narrow answer possible.

Second, write your standing rules for responding to the institution, in advance and in a calm moment: I will keep important exchanges in writing, answer only specific points factually, decline to defend my character, run everything past the imagined third reader, and take my feelings elsewhere. Rules set in advance are far easier to keep than decisions made under the pressure of an accusation.

Third, name where your feeling will go when a communication lands: the person you will call, the advocate you will consult, the page you will write, before you touch the response. Deciding this ahead of time is what makes the measured response survivable, because you are not asking yourself to swallow an unbearable feeling, only to move it somewhere better.

Fourth, the next time you find yourself composing a long defense to the institution, write it in full, and then do not send it. Put everything into it, the whole history, the corrections, the plea to be believed, and let the writing discharge the feeling, then save it somewhere private or delete it. What you send, if anything, is the narrow, factual, on-the-record response that a fair third reader would find reasonable. Separating the writing that heals you from the response that goes on the record is how you get the relief of full expression without handing the process the material it feeds on.

What to carry forward

Answer the process and not the shame: address the specific, answerable points factually and on the record, and decline the character attack, because the attack is not a question but a hook the reversal uses to pull you into producing more material. Keep important exchanges in writing and on the record, following up meetings with your own written account, because the spoken word can be denied and the official record shaped, while the measured written word is protection. Write everything for the fair third reader, so that what you commit to the record is only ever what a neutral observer would find reasonable, which strips out the heat the reversal wants to quote against you. Route the real emotional pressure elsewhere, to a friend, an advocate, a therapist, or a private page, so the record stays measured while your feeling is fully honored somewhere it can do some good. Having learned to answer the process without feeding it, the next chapter turns to the hardest release of all, the hope that the institution will one day admit what it did.

Chapter 8: The Vindication That Never Comes

Lorien waited nine years for the letter that would say she had been right. She was forty-eight, and she had reported serious safeguarding failures at the organization where she worked, and been forced out for it, and in the years since she had held on to a private certainty: that one day the truth would come out, that the organization would be exposed, that someone in authority would finally acknowledge that Lorien had been right and had been wronged. She read every news story about the sector hoping this would be the scandal that vindicated her. She kept her files ready for the inquiry that would surely come. She structured a great deal of her inner life around a future moment of vindication, and that moment did not arrive. The organization carried on. The people who had forced her out were promoted. And Lorien slowly understood that she had been waiting at a door for a visitor who was never going to come, and that her life had been passing while she waited.

This chapter is about the deepest tie in the whole ordeal and the hardest to release: the hope that the institution will one day admit what it did, that you will be vindicated, that the truth will come out and your name will be cleared. It is the hope that keeps you tethered to the institution long after you have left it, checking for the news that will vindicate you, waiting for the acknowledgment that will make it right. Releasing this hope is not the same as deciding you were wrong, or giving up on justice. It is recognizing that the specific vindication you are waiting for usually does not come, and that your peace cannot be built on an acknowledgment the institution is structured never to give. This is a grief, and moving through it is one of the most freeing things you will do.

The vindication that never comes

The principle of this chapter is that you cannot build your peace on a vindication that usually never comes. Something in you insists that the story is not over until the institution admits what it did, until you are publicly cleared, until the truth is acknowledged by the body that denied it. And so you keep waiting, keep checking, keep your hope fixed on a future reckoning, because to release it would feel like accepting the institution's verdict. But the vindication you are waiting for requires the institution to do the one thing the reversal is built to prevent: to acknowledge that it harmed you and that its account was false. That acknowledgment is precisely what the whole tactic is built to avoid, which means the vindication is not merely delayed. It is structurally unlikely, and building your peace on it is building on ground that may never hold.

Releasing the hope does not mean deciding the institution was right or that no justice is ever possible. Some people do receive vindication, through legal processes, external investigations, or the slow turning of events, and where a genuine avenue to justice is open, pursuing it can be right, as a later chapter discusses. But the inner work of this chapter is separate from any external avenue: it is releasing the requirement that the institution acknowledge what it did in order for you to be at peace, because that requirement hands your peace to a body committed never to grant it. When you stop waiting at the door, you are not giving up on justice or on your life; you are refusing to let your recovery depend on an acknowledgment that may never come.

Why the acknowledgment will not come

It is worth being precise about why the acknowledgment usually will not arrive, because the hope regrows unless you pull it up by the root. For the institution to acknowledge you in the way you long for, it would have to admit that it harmed you and that its version of events reversed the truth, and that admission is the exact thing the reversal is designed to prevent. The whole tactic is a defense against accountability, and granting you the acknowledgment you seek would mean surrendering that defense, accepting liability, embarrassment, and cost, which the institution is structured never to do (Freyd, 1997). You are not waiting for a body that has simply not yet gotten around to admitting the truth; you are waiting for a body whose entire strategy depends on never admitting it.

This is why your hope that the next inquiry, the next news story, the next change of leadership will finally bring the acknowledgment so often disappoints. The obstacle was never that the institution lacked the information or the occasion; it lacks the will, because admitting the wrong would cost it more than maintaining the reversal. New leadership inherits the institution's interest in not reopening old liabilities; new inquiries are often scoped to avoid exactly the admission you seek. Lorien had believed for years that the truth would surely come out, and the release came when she understood that the institution's silence was not a gap waiting to be filled but a position being actively maintained, and that no scandal or inquiry was likely to force from it the acknowledgment it was structured to withhold.

The trap of the life on hold

The hope for vindication carries a particular danger that the hope in earlier chapters does not, and it is worth naming plainly: it can put your entire life on hold. While you are waiting to be vindicated, you may find yourself unable to move on, unable to build the next chapter of your life, because moving on can feel like giving up the fight, like conceding that the acknowledgment will not come. So you stay tethered to the institution and the injustice, checking, waiting, keeping the files ready, and the years pass while you wait for a reckoning that does not arrive. The waiting itself becomes a second harm, a way the institution continues to take from you long after you have left it, because your unlived life is part of what the reversal costs you.

Seeing this is what makes release feel less like surrender and more like reclamation. To release the hope of vindication is not to abandon the truth of what happened; you can know, with complete certainty, that you were right and were wronged, and still stop waiting for the institution to say so. What you release is the requirement that the institution acknowledge it before you allow yourself to live, and releasing that requirement is what lets you take your life back from a body that would otherwise hold it hostage. Lorien realized that the organization had taken her job, and that by waiting nine years for its acknowledgment she had let it take nine years of her life as well, and that the one thing still in her power was to stop letting it take any more.

The closure you give yourself

The vindication you were waiting for from the institution may not come, but there is another closure that does not depend on it: the closure you give yourself, by reaching your own clear conclusion, releasing the impossible requirement, and turning toward your life. It is a quieter closure than the public vindication you imagined, and it does not require the institution's participation, which is exactly what makes it reliable, because no one else holds the key to it. You will grieve, and you can also, alongside the grief, extend to yourself the acknowledgment you were waiting for the institution to give: recognizing, in your own account, that you reported a real wrong, that you were right to do so, and that the institution's turning on you was its failure and not your fault.

This self-given closure is not a consolation prize; it is the only closure that was ever truly available, because the institution's acknowledgment was always outside your control and always unlikely. When you give yourself the recognition you were waiting for, you move the source of your peace from a body committed to withholding it to yourself, who can grant it, and that transfer is the moment your recovery stops depending on the one party guaranteed not to help. Lorien never received the letter she had waited nine years for. What she received instead was the day she stopped needing it, and gave herself the recognition she had been waiting for the organization to provide, and found that it held, because it did not depend on a body committed never to offer it.

There is a strange freedom in this that does not look like freedom from outside. Waiting for vindication feels like keeping faith with the truth, and releasing it feels like a loss, but the truth runs the other way. As long as your peace depends on the institution admitting what it did, the institution holds the key to your peace, and a body committed to the reversal will never turn it. Releasing the requirement takes the key back. It moves the source of your recovery from a body that will not act to the one person who can, namely you, and that transfer, painful as it is, is the moment your healing stops waiting on the party guaranteed never to help.

Hoovering by the institution

The hope for vindication is not only a private ache; it can be a handle the institution uses to keep you engaged on its terms, and recognizing this protects you from being pulled back. When you begin to move on, an institution sometimes offers just enough to reactivate the hope: a hint that your case might be reviewed, a partial and heavily qualified acknowledgment, a settlement discussion that seems to promise recognition, an appeal process that dangles the possibility of being cleared. These overtures can arrive precisely when you were finding distance, and they work by reawakening the hope that this time you will finally be vindicated, pulling you back into the institution's orbit and its timeline.

Understanding this lets you meet such overtures without being captured. When the partial acknowledgment or the review or the settlement talk arrives, you can weigh it clearly on its merits, with proper advice where it matters, without letting it reactivate the whole fantasy of full vindication. A settlement may be worth taking for practical reasons; a review may be worth engaging for concrete ones. But you engage with the actual, limited thing on offer, not with the hope of total acknowledgment it seems to promise, because that hope is exactly what keeps you tethered. Lorien learned that the organization's occasional gestures toward reopening her case reliably came when she was pulling away, and reliably led nowhere, which taught her to weigh each gesture for what it concretely was rather than for the vindication it seemed to dangle.

When there is a real avenue to justice

Releasing the hope of the institution's acknowledgment does not mean abandoning any real avenue to justice that may be open to you, and it is worth holding the two apart clearly. There are genuine external routes, a legal claim, a regulator, an ombudsman, an external inquiry, a professional oversight body, that sometimes do deliver a measure of vindication or remedy, and pursuing an appropriate one, with proper advice, can be entirely right. The next chapter on the decision to stay, leave, or pursue takes this up in full. The inner release of this chapter is not an argument against pursuing justice through real channels; it is an argument against staking your peace on an outcome you do not control.

The distinction is between action and dependence. You can pursue a genuine avenue to justice as a considered action, doing what is in your power and then releasing the result, which is very different from suspending your whole life on the hope of vindication. The healthiest position holds both: pursue what is worth pursuing through proper channels, and simultaneously release the requirement that any of it succeed before you allow yourself to recover and live. Lorien eventually pursued one external route that was genuinely open to her, and did so from a place of released hope rather than desperate waiting, which meant that when it delivered only a partial result, she was disappointed but not destroyed, because her peace had never been staked on it in the first place.

Trying it on your own situation

Begin releasing the hope and finding your own closure.

First, write down the vindication you keep waiting for: the admission, the exposure, the public clearing of your name you have been hoping the institution or events will one day deliver. Then write beside it, plainly, why it is unlikely to come, because giving it would mean the institution surrendering the reversal. Naming the unlikelihood is how the release begins.

Second, notice the ways the waiting has put your life on hold: the checking, the files kept ready, the next chapter of your life postponed until vindication arrives. Name one part of your life you have been keeping on hold, and take one step to reclaim it, because your unlived life is part of what the waiting costs you.

Third, give yourself, in writing, the recognition you have been waiting for the institution to give. Set down your own clear account: that you reported a real wrong, that you were right to do so, and that the institution's turning on you was its failure and not your fault. The closure you author does not require the institution, which is what makes it reliable.

Fourth, hold action and dependence apart. If there is a genuine external avenue to justice open to you, a legal claim, a regulator, an ombudsman, an oversight body, weigh pursuing it with proper advice, as a considered action. But make the decision to pursue it separately from the decision to release your peace, so that you do what is in your power and then let go of the result, rather than suspending your recovery on an outcome you do not control. Pursue what is worth pursuing, and stake your peace on none of it.

What to carry forward

You cannot build your peace on a vindication that usually never comes, because the acknowledgment you are waiting for requires the institution to admit the harm and surrender its false account, which is the exact thing the reversal is built to prevent (Freyd, 1997). Your hope that the next inquiry or change of leadership will bring it so often disappoints because the obstacle is not information or occasion but the institution's will, since admitting the wrong would cost it more than maintaining the reversal. The hope for vindication carries a particular danger, that it puts your whole life on hold while you wait, so that your unlived life becomes a second harm the reversal inflicts, which is why release is reclamation rather than surrender. You can know with complete certainty that you were right and were wronged and still release the requirement that the institution say so, giving yourself the acknowledgment it will not, which moves the source of your peace to the one person who can grant it. Having released the institution, the next chapter turns toward the people who still stand with you and the community you can build.

Chapter 9: The People Who Still Stand With You

Maevren lost most of a professional world and kept two people, and it took a long time to understand that the two were worth more than the world. They were forty-one, and when the institution turned on them for reporting a manager's misconduct, the losses came fast: the team they had led, the colleagues they ate lunch with, the professional network built over fifteen years, the invitations, the standing. For a while Maevren could see only the emptiness, the calls that stopped coming, the sense of having been erased from a community that had been most of their adult life. They almost missed the two who remained: one former colleague who had left the organization years before and simply did not believe the story, and one person from outside the field entirely who had watched the whole thing and never wavered. Those two, Maevren eventually understood, were not the remnant of a lost world. They were the beginning of a smaller, truer one.

This chapter is about the people who still stand with you, and about the community you can build when the professional world you belonged to has closed against you. Being turned on by an institution often means losing not one relationship but a whole network at once, and the isolation that follows is real and severe. But the answer to that isolation is not to win back the community that turned, which is usually impossible and always exhausting. It is to find, keep, and tend the few who did not turn, and to build, deliberately, a community of connection that the reversal cannot reach. Those few, and the community you choose, are worth more than the network you lost, and building your life around them is one of the wisest things you can do.

The people who still stand with you

The principle of this chapter is that a few people who stand with you outweigh a professional world that turned. When you lose the community you belonged to, the natural focus is on the loss, on everyone who believed the institution or fell silent, and on the particular grief of losing not individuals but a whole world at once. That focus, though understandable, keeps you oriented toward what you cannot control and cannot recover. The wiser orientation is toward the few who remained and the connections you can still build, because those are the relationships that can actually sustain you, reflect your real self back to you, and give you the belonging the institution withdrew.

This reframing matters because your energy is finite, and a long recovery will demand most of it. Poured into trying to win back a community that turned, that energy mostly evaporates. Invested in the few who stand with you and the community you are building, it compounds, deepening the relationships that are keeping you upright. The institution took the belonging you had earned and made it conditional on your silence. The people who stand with you offer belonging on truthful terms, for who you actually are, and that is not a lesser thing than what you lost. It is, in many ways, sturdier, because it does not depend on your staying useful to an institution.

Why the isolation is part of the tactic

Understanding that the isolation is not incidental changes how you respond to it. The reversal isolates you partly to build a chorus and partly to strip you of support, because a person cut off from their people is easier to overwhelm, easier to discredit, and easier to convince of their own guilt. Isolation is not a sad byproduct of being turned on; it serves the reversal. Recovery and resilience depend heavily on connection, and a person deprived of support is far more vulnerable to being broken down (Herman, 1992). The loss of your community is doing something that serves the institution, and your isolation is not a verdict on your worth but a consequence of the tactic working as designed.

Seeing the isolation as a feature rather than a judgment changes its meaning. Each colleague who fell away is not necessarily delivering a verdict on your character; many are people who heard the institution's confident story, had their own reasons to accept it or their own fear of standing with you, and did what people in institutions do, which is protect themselves. That is a painful fact about institutions, and it is usually not the moral judgment it feels like. Reframing the losses this way does not remove the grief, but it removes the extra layer of self-condemnation, the sense that so many people falling away must mean the institution was right about you. It does not mean that. It means the tactic did what it was built to do, and it did it to your relationships, not because of your guilt.

Tending the few and the value of outside witnesses

The few who remain need tending, not because they are fragile but because relationships that sustain you through a long ordeal deserve care rather than being taken for granted. This means reaching out to them, and not only when you are in crisis and need something, but simply to stay connected, so the relationship remains a relationship and not only a lifeline. It means, where you can, letting them see what you are going through without making every interaction about the institution, so the connection stays a place of ordinary human warmth and not only a refuge. And it means receiving their view of you, letting their steady sight of your real character be a counterweight to the institution's story, rather than deflecting it because you cannot yet believe it.

There is particular value in people outside the institution, who hold a view of you that the institution's account cannot reach. A friend from another part of your life, a former colleague who left long ago, a person from outside the field entirely, sees you whole, apart from the story the institution has built, and their view is a kind of evidence that the villain portrait is false. Maevren found that the friend from outside the field did more to steady them than any argument they could make to themselves, because that friend was not weighing the institution's case against Maevren's; they simply knew Maevren, plainly and from years of ordinary life, as a person who bore no resemblance to the troublemaker the institution described. People who see you from outside the institution's frame are living proof that the frame is not the truth of you.

Building a community and connection as resistance

Beyond the few who remain, there is the community you can build, and it is worth saying plainly that a chosen community is a real one, not a substitute. New colleagues in a new setting, people met through the very experience you went through, friends who become as close as family, a network rebuilt on different ground, these are not a consolation prize. For many people turned on by an institution, they become the first experience of professional and personal belonging that does not depend on staying silent, and that belonging can be sturdier than what was lost, because it is not held hostage to an institution's comfort. Building a new community is not settling for less; it is often finding belonging on better terms than you had before.

It also helps to see that keeping and building these connections is a form of quiet resistance to the reversal. The tactic wants you isolated, doubting, and cut off from any reflection of your real self. Every real connection you maintain works directly against that aim: it keeps a true mirror in your life, it denies the reversal the total isolation it seeks, and it reminds you, through ordinary human contact, that you are a person who is known and valued, not the figure the institution's story describes. On the days when the isolating voice is loudest and tells you to withdraw, that you are too much trouble, that people are better off without you, reaching out anyway is a move against the reversal, because your withdrawal is exactly what it wants. Maevren came to treat contact with the two who remained, and later with the new community they slowly built, almost as a discipline, reaching out especially on the days the old voice said they were toxic, because the reaching out was the counter-argument, made not in words but in the simple fact of remaining connected to people who saw them truly.

When trusting anyone feels dangerous

There is a complication that catches many people turned on by an institution, and it deserves naming: after being betrayed by a body you trusted and abandoned by colleagues you relied on, trusting anyone can feel dangerous, even the few who stood with you and the new people who offer connection. The betrayal at the heart of the experience, and the desertion that followed, can leave you scanning even loyal people for the signs that they, too, will eventually turn or fall away. This wariness is understandable, a natural bruise left by what happened, but if it goes unrecognized it can push away the very people trying to stay, and keep you isolated long after the institution is out of your life.

Go gently with yourself here, and gently with them. You do not have to trust all at once, and you do not have to explain the wariness away. It is enough to notice it, to name it inwardly as a bruise rather than a truth about these particular people, and to let the few and the new earn your trust slowly through their steadiness, which they generally will if you give them the chance. The institution damaged your capacity to trust along with everything else, and part of recovery is letting safe people be safe again, at whatever pace you can manage. Maevren had to consciously stop testing the two who remained for signs of desertion, and found that once they let the steadiness register instead of bracing against it, those relationships became the ground they had never had at the institution, not because the two were perfect, but because Maevren finally let themselves be held.

The particular loss of a working identity

There is a specific dimension to this loss worth naming, because it is easy to underestimate: for many people, a professional community is not only a source of relationships but a large part of their identity, and losing it can feel like losing a piece of who they are. If your work was central to your sense of yourself, then being cast out of your professional world is not only the loss of colleagues and standing but a blow to your identity, a sudden uncertainty about who you are if you are no longer the person you were within that institution. This is part of why the loss cuts so deep, and naming it helps you understand your own devastation rather than judging it as an overreaction to mere workplace trouble.

The people who stand with you help here in a particular way, because they knew you as more than your role. The friend from outside the field, the colleague who left long ago, the person who values you apart from your professional standing, reflects back a self that was never only your position at the institution, and that reflection is part of how you begin to recover an identity larger than the role you lost. You are not only what the institution made you or took from you; you are a person with a character and a life that predate and outlast the institution, and the people who see that are living evidence of it. Maevren, who had poured most of themselves into their work, had to rediscover a self that stood apart from the institution, and the two who stood with them were exactly the ones who had always seen that larger self, which was why their steadiness did so much to restore it.

Trying it on your own situation

Turn toward the people who stand with you and the community you can build.

First, make two lists, but linger on the second. On one, the relationships the reversal cost you, so you can grieve them fully. On the other, the few who did not turn, who still see your real self, even one or two, including anyone who knows you from outside the institution. These are the people this chapter is about, and they are where your energy belongs.

Second, reach out to one of them this week, not in crisis and not to discuss the institution, but simply to stay connected as people who care about each other. Tending the relationship in ordinary times, and not only hard ones, is the practice.

Third, name one connection you could build or deepen toward a new community: a new professional setting, a group of people who went through something similar, a person who has offered belonging apart from the institution. Then take one small step toward it, because a new community is built the same way any is, through showing up over time.

Fourth, when you notice yourself testing a loyal person for signs they will turn or abandon you, name the reflex for what it is: a bruise from the institution, not a truth about this person. You do not have to trust all at once, and you do not have to force it. Let the steadiness of a safe person register, one interaction at a time, instead of bracing against it, and let them earn your trust at whatever pace you can manage. Relearning trust after an institutional betrayal is slow work, and going gently with it, rather than either forcing trust or refusing it, is how the few and the new become the ground you never had.

What to carry forward

A few people who stand with you outweigh a professional world that turned, because those relationships can sustain you and offer belonging on truthful terms, while trying to win back the community that closed against you mostly drains the energy your recovery needs. The isolation is part of the tactic, not a verdict on your worth, because a person cut off from support is easier to overwhelm and convince of their own guilt (Herman, 1992), which means each lost colleague is usually the tactic working, not proof the institution was right. Tend the few who remain, especially those who see you from outside the institution's frame and hold a view its account cannot reach, and build a new community that is a real one and often belonging on better terms than you had. Every connection you keep is quiet resistance to a reversal that wants you isolated, which is why reaching out, especially when the old voice says you are too much trouble, is a move toward recovery. With people around you who see you truly, the next chapter turns to surviving the prolonged process itself, and keeping your body and mind through it.

Chapter 10: Surviving the Process

Orlian could not eat on the mornings of the meetings. He was fifty, an accountant who had reported financial irregularities and then spent fourteen months as the subject of an investigation, and long before each scheduled meeting his body would begin to fail him: the sleepless nights, the churning stomach, the racing heart, the dread that started days in advance and did not lift until the meeting was over, at which point a new dread began for the next one. He was a competent, steady man in every other part of his life, and the process reduced him, month after month, to a state of constant physical alarm. He thought there was something wrong with him, that he was weak, that a stronger person would have handled it better. What Orlian did not understand, until he learned how threat works in the body, was that his reaction was not weakness but physiology, the predictable response of a nervous system under a prolonged threat it could neither fight nor escape, and that surviving the process would require him to tend his body, not just his case.

This chapter is about surviving the process itself, the prolonged investigation, the drawn-out proceedings, the months or years of being the subject of an institution's machinery. This is not only a legal or practical ordeal; it is a physical and psychological one, a sustained assault on the body and mind that can wear down even the strongest person. The institution's process is often slow, and that slowness is itself part of the toll, keeping you in a state of alarm for months on end. Learning to survive the process means learning to tend your body and mind through it, so that the prolonged threat does not break you before the matter is resolved, and so that you do not, in your exhaustion, supply the reactions the reversal is waiting for.

Surviving the process

The principle of this chapter is that surviving the process requires tending your body and mind, not only managing your case. A prolonged institutional process is a sustained threat, and a sustained threat takes a physical toll: disrupted sleep, appetite, and concentration, a body kept in a state of alarm for far longer than it was built to sustain. If you treat the ordeal as purely a matter of arguments and evidence and neglect the toll on your body and mind, you risk being worn down to the point where you cannot think clearly, cannot respond well, and cannot outlast a process designed to outlast you. Tending your body and mind is not a distraction from surviving the process; it is central to surviving it.

This reframing matters because people in your position often neglect exactly this, pouring everything into the case and treating their own physical and psychological collapse as an unimportant side effect. It is not unimportant; it is the mechanism by which prolonged processes defeat people, not by winning the argument but by exhausting the person until they give up, break down, or react in a way that damages them. Recognizing that your survival depends on tending yourself, and not only on tending your case, is what lets you last, and lasting is often what the situation requires, because these processes are frequently won or lost on endurance rather than merits. Orlian came to understand that his body was not a distraction from the fight but the ground on which the fight would be won or lost, and that keeping himself functioning was as strategic as any response he wrote.

Why the dread is physiology, not weakness

It is worth understanding why the process affects your body so powerfully, because understanding it removes the shame that makes the toll heavier. A threat, especially a sustained and inescapable one, activates the body's threat response, a physiological state that prepares you to fight or flee, flooding you with the alarm you feel before a meeting, disrupting sleep and digestion, keeping the whole system braced. This response is automatic and largely outside conscious control, driven by systems far older and faster than deliberate thought (Porges, 2011). The dread you feel is not a sign of weakness or a failure of character; it is your nervous system responding to a real threat exactly as it is built to, and the fact that the threat is bureaucratic rather than physical does not change how the body reads it.

This is compounded by the particular cruelty of an institutional threat, which is often prolonged and inescapable in a way that keeps the threat response switched on for months. The body is built to handle acute threats that resolve quickly, not a threat that persists for a year, and sustained activation of this kind wears the system down, held as it is in the body over time (van der Kolk, 2014). If you are exhausted, sleepless, unable to concentrate, and flooded with dread, this is why: you are a system built for short threats being subjected to a long one. That is not weakness, and treating it as weakness only adds shame to exhaustion. Orlian stopped believing he was weak once he understood that fourteen months of sustained threat would wear down anyone's body, and that his physical state was a measure of the ordeal's length, not of his character.

Tending the body through a long threat

Because the toll is physical, much of surviving the process is physical too, and a few practices make a real difference. Protect your sleep as far as you can, because sleep is where the body recovers and its loss accelerates everything else; even partial protection of your sleep is worth the effort. Keep your body moving, because physical activity discharges some of the activation the threat generates and gives the alarm somewhere to go. Use the settling practices that speak to the nervous system directly, particularly slow breathing with a longer exhale than inhale, which signals to the body that the immediate threat has passed and helps bring the system down from alarm (Porges, 2011). None of this resolves the case, but all of it keeps you functioning through the case, which is the point.

Around the acute moments, the meetings and the deadlines, tend yourself deliberately. Before a dreaded meeting, use the settling practices; afterward, do something that discharges the activation and returns you to your life, rather than sitting in the aftermath replaying it. Structure your life so that the process does not occupy every hour, because a threat that fills all your time and attention wears you down faster than one you can step away from. Orlian learned to walk for an hour after every meeting, to breathe slowly in the parked car before going in, and to keep parts of his week entirely free of the case, and these physical practices did more to keep him functioning across fourteen months than any amount of willpower had, because they worked with his body instead of demanding it simply endure.

Not collapsing and not exploding

The prolonged threat pushes toward two failures, and knowing them helps you avoid both: collapse and explosion. Under sustained pressure, some people collapse, becoming unable to respond, missing deadlines, withdrawing into a shutdown that the process then reads against them; others explode, reacting to the provocation of the process with an outburst that becomes fresh evidence. Both are understandable responses to sustained threat, and both tend to damage you, which is why the aim is to stay in the functioning middle, neither shutting down nor blowing up, for as long as the process requires. This is not a matter of willpower by itself; it is a matter of tending your body and mind so that you have the reserves to stay in that middle.

Self-compassion is central here, because the person who meets their own exhaustion and fear with harsh self-judgment burns through their reserves faster, while the person who treats their own struggle with kindness sustains themselves better across a long ordeal (Neff,

2003). You will have bad days in a long process, days you handle poorly, days the dread wins; meeting those days with contempt only deepens the collapse, while meeting them with the understanding you would offer anyone under sustained threat helps you recover and continue. The goal was never to be superhuman across months of pressure, which no one can be, but to tend yourself well enough to stay functioning through it, forgiving the bad days and returning to the practices. Orlian found that treating himself kindly on the worst days, rather than adding self-contempt to his exhaustion, was what let him last the fourteen months without either collapsing or exploding, because kindness kept his reserves from running out.

The weaponized slowness

There is a feature of institutional processes worth naming directly, because it feels like incompetence and is often something closer to strategy: the slowness. Investigations drag on for months, decisions are deferred, deadlines pass without resolution, and you are left suspended, unable to move forward and unable to put it down. This slowness is not always deliberate, but its effect serves the institution regardless of intent, because a person kept suspended in uncertainty for a year is worn down, drained of resources and resolve, and more likely to give up or settle than one facing a swift resolution. The delay itself is part of the toll, and sometimes part of the tactic, whether or not anyone designed it that way.

Understanding this protects you from two errors. The first is taking the slowness personally, reading each delay as a fresh catastrophe or a sign of some new development, when it is often just the process grinding at its usual pace. The second is letting the slowness set the tempo of your entire life, so that you live suspended, holding your breath between one deferred deadline and the next. The defense against a slow process is to refuse to live suspended within it: to build a life alongside the process that continues regardless of its pace, so that the institution's delays do not command every month of your life. Orlian learned to stop reading each delay as meaningful and to keep living his life in the long gaps, because a process that might take two years could not be allowed to put two years of his life on hold, and declining to be suspended was itself a way of surviving.

Get the support the process requires

Surviving a prolonged process is not something you should attempt with willpower and breathing by yourself, and it is worth saying plainly that this is a situation in which support matters and seeking it is wisdom, not weakness. Practical support, a lawyer, an advocate, a union representative, someone who knows how these processes work, can carry part of the burden you have been carrying by yourself, and having a knowledgeable person handling the procedural fight frees some of your resources for simply surviving. Emotional and psychological support matters just as much: a therapist who understands what a prolonged institutional threat does to a person can help you hold the dread and the exhaustion, and the people who stand with you can share the weight that is otherwise yours to bear by yourself.

If the process is affecting you severely, if you cannot sleep for extended periods, if the dread has become unrelenting, if you find yourself unable to function or experiencing thoughts of harming yourself, that is a clear signal to seek professional help without delay, both for your survival and because a person supported through the ordeal fares far better than one enduring it in isolation. There is no failure in needing help to survive a sustained assault on your body and mind; there would only be unnecessary suffering in refusing it. Orlian eventually brought in both a lawyer for the case and a therapist for himself, and found that sharing the burden across people who knew what they were doing was what finally made the fourteen months survivable, because no one is built to carry a threat that long entirely on their own.

Trying it on your own situation

Tend your body and mind so you can survive the process.

First, name the physical toll the process is taking: your sleep, your appetite, your concentration, the dread before meetings. Naming it as physiology, the predictable response of a nervous system under prolonged threat, is what removes the shame that makes the toll heavier.

Second, adopt two or three physical practices and hold to them: protect your sleep as far as you can, keep your body moving, and use slow breathing with a long exhale before and after the acute moments. These work with your body to keep you functioning across a long ordeal, which is what surviving the process requires.

Third, decide in advance how you will treat yourself on the bad days, because in a long process they will come. Meet your own exhaustion and fear with the kindness you would offer anyone under sustained threat, rather than the contempt that burns through your reserves. Kindness on the hard days is what keeps you in the functioning middle, neither collapsing nor exploding.

Fourth, get the support the process requires, and build a life alongside it. Name the practical support you could bring in, a lawyer, an advocate, a union representative, and the emotional support you could lean on, a therapist and the people who stand with you, so that you are not carrying a threat this long entirely by yourself. Then name one part of your life you will keep alive regardless of the process, so its slowness does not command every month, and if the toll becomes severe, if you cannot sleep for long stretches, if the dread is unrelenting, or if you have thoughts of harming yourself, treat that as a clear reason to seek professional help without delay.

What to carry forward

Surviving the process requires tending your body and mind, not only managing your case, because a prolonged institutional process is a sustained threat that wears people down until they collapse, break, or react, which is how these processes defeat people regardless of the merits. The dread and exhaustion are physiology, not weakness, the automatic response of a nervous system to a real threat (Porges, 2011), compounded by the unusual cruelty of a threat that persists for months and is held in the body over time (van der Kolk, 2014). Tend the body directly, protecting sleep, keeping moving, and using slow breathing with a long exhale, because the toll is physical and so much of surviving it is physical too. Aim for the functioning middle, neither collapsing nor exploding, and meet the bad days with self-compassion rather than contempt, since kindness sustains your reserves across a long ordeal while harsh judgment burns them (Neff, 2003). Having learned to survive the process, the next chapter turns to the reader who made a genuine mistake, and how to own it without accepting the institution's frame.

Chapter 11: Own Your Part, Refuse the Frame

Sevrin almost let a real mistake swallow her whole case. She was forty-four, a manager who had reported serious wrongdoing by a director, and in the course of raising it she had done one thing that was genuinely wrong: she had accessed a document she was not authorized to access, to gather evidence, and she knew it had been a mistake. It was real, and she owned that it was real. But by the time the institution had finished, that single unauthorized access had become the whole story: not the wrongdoing she reported, but her breach, her misconduct, her supposed bad character. And Sevrin found herself trapped, because every time she tried to defend herself, she ran into the true thing she had done, and it felt as though owning that one real mistake meant conceding the institution's entire frame, that she was the wrongdoer and the director the victim. So she froze, unable to own the real part without seeming to accept the false whole. This chapter is about the way out of that trap, and it is one of the most important in the book, because it is where accountability and self-respect finally stop being enemies.

Everything so far has helped you refuse a false frame and survive it. This chapter addresses the harder and more particular situation of the reader who made a genuine mistake, who has a real thing to own. If that is you, this chapter is written with special care, because your situation is both more complicated and more hopeful than it feels. You can own what is genuinely yours, cleanly and fully, without accepting the false frame the institution has built around it, and learning to do exactly that is what frees you from a trap that holds many people who were, in part, in the wrong. Owning your part and refusing the frame is the mature ground on which the rest of your recovery stands.

Own the part, refuse the frame

The principle of this chapter is to own the part and refuse the frame. The trap that catches people who made a real mistake is all-or-nothing thinking, the belief that admitting any fault means admitting the institution's whole case, that owning one true thing concedes the entire false frame. This belief is false, and it is also paralyzing, because it forces an impossible choice between two lies: deny everything, including what is true, or accept everything, including the institution's frame that you were the real wrongdoer. The way out is to reject the all-or-nothing frame entirely, and to hold two things at once: yes, I did this specific thing and it was wrong, and no, that does not make me the wrongdoer the institution describes or mean the wrong I reported was not real.

This is harder than either pure denial or pure surrender, and it is the only truthful path for a reader who genuinely made a mistake. It requires you to separate your real fault, which you will own, from the false frame, which you will refuse, and to hold that separation steadily even as the institution insists the two are one. The two lists you built in the self-check chapter are exactly this separation made concrete. Owning the part and refusing the frame is what lets you be both accountable and self-respecting, which is a combination the all-or-nothing frame says is impossible and which is, in fact, the truth about almost anyone who ever handled a hard situation imperfectly.

Why owning a fault does not concede the frame

It is worth seeing clearly why admitting a real fault does not, in logic or in truth, concede the institution's whole frame, because the fear that it does is what keeps people trapped. A specific mistake is a specific mistake. That you accessed a document you should not have, or worded something badly, or skipped a required step, is a fact about that particular act. It is not, by itself, evidence that you were the real wrongdoer or that the wrong you reported was not real, because a single fault, even a serious one, does not transform you into the villain of the story or transform the wrongdoer into the victim. The institution needs you to believe that your one true fault proves its whole frame, but the logic does not hold: a person can make a real mistake, even a serious one, and still have reported a genuine wrong and been reversed for it.

This matters because the reversal specifically exploits your conscience. A person with a conscience, confronted with a genuine fault, feels the pull to accept responsibility, and the reversal uses that pull, attaching the whole false frame to the true fault so that your genuine accountability drags the entire false story in behind it. The defense is not to abandon your conscience and deny the fault, which corrupts you and helps nothing. The defense is to give your conscience a precise target: own exactly what is true, no more, and refuse to let the owning extend one inch into the frame. Your integrity is served by owning the real fault. It is not served by accepting a false story about who was the wrongdoer, which is not integrity at all but its counterfeit.

Genuine accountability, cleanly done

Where you made a real mistake, genuine accountability is not only possible but healthy, and it is worth doing well, both because it is right and because it strengthens rather than weakens your position. Genuine accountability has a shape: it names the specific thing clearly, without minimizing and without the vague non-admission that concedes nothing, it takes responsibility for that specific thing without the reflexive shifting of blame, and it does not concede anything beyond the actual fault. You own what you did because it is right, cleanly and specifically, and you stop precisely at the edge of what you actually did, letting the real fault be exactly its own size and no larger.

The crucial discipline is that genuine accountability for the real part is kept entirely separate from the false frame. Sevrin could say, clearly, I accessed a document I was not authorized to access, and that was wrong, without in the same breath accepting that she was the real wrongdoer and the director the victim. Indeed, the cleanness of owning the real fault often clarifies the falseness of the rest, because a specific, sincere accountability for a specific act stands in sharp contrast to the sweeping frame the reversal imposes. When Sevrin finally owned the unauthorized access plainly, without defending it and without letting it swallow the rest, she found that the clean admission actually strengthened her ability to refuse the false frame, because it demonstrated, to herself most of all, that she was a person who owned her real faults and precisely for that reason did not need to accept invented ones. Counterintuitively, owning the real mistake cleanly made her more credible, not less, because a person who admits a genuine fault reads as truthful in a way that a person who denies everything never can.

The mistake you own versus the confession the institution wants

A caution is essential here, because the institution can also weaponize the language of accountability, and you must be able to tell genuine accountability from the false confession it is angling for. Genuine accountability is specific, proportionate, and freely given; it owns a real, identifiable act at its real size. The false confession the reversal seeks is different: it is a sweeping admission that you were the wrongdoer, that the wrong you reported was not real, that the whole frame is true, extracted under pressure and used immediately as final proof of the story. The institution may push you toward this false confession, often bundled into a settlement or a resignation, insisting that real accountability means admitting you were the problem, that anything less is denial. It is not. Admitting to being the wrongdoer when you reported a genuine wrong is not accountability; it is capitulation to the reversal wearing accountability's clothes.

The test is whether the admission is true and specific, or false and sweeping. Owning that you accessed the document is genuine accountability. Signing a statement that you were the real wrongdoer and the director did nothing amiss, when the wrong you reported was real, is the false confession, and you should refuse it as firmly as you own the real fault. This becomes acute in settlements and negotiated exits, where institutions frequently require, as a condition, that you accept fault or sign away your account, and where you may face real pressure to do so. Weigh such terms carefully and with proper advice, and know that owning your genuine mistake never requires you to confess to the institution's whole false frame. Where a settlement is worth taking for practical reasons, taking it need not mean believing the frame; you can accept a practical resolution while privately holding, and recording for yourself, the truth of what actually happened (Neff, 2003).

The exit that demands a confession

There is a particular version of the false confession worth naming, because it is so common in institutional endings: the negotiated exit that is offered only on the condition that you accept fault. The institution may be willing to let you leave with a settlement, a reference, or an end to the process, but only if you sign a statement admitting you were the problem, withdraw your report, or agree to say nothing about what happened. The offer can be tempting, because it promises an end to an ordeal that has consumed you, and all it seems to ask is a signature. It is a trap in a particular way, because the price of the ending is the surrender of the truth about your own conduct, and sometimes the abandonment of the very wrong you reported.

You can weigh such an offer clearly, with proper advice, without letting the exhaustion of the process make the decision for you. Sometimes a settlement is genuinely worth taking, for financial security, for an end to the toll, for the chance to move on, and taking it does not require you to believe the confession you may have to sign for practical reasons. What matters is that you know the difference between a practical resolution and a true admission, so that whatever you sign to end the ordeal, you hold privately and record for yourself the truth of what actually happened, and do not let a document signed under pressure become your own account of your life. Sevrin was eventually offered exactly such an exit, and she took a version of it on her lawyer's advice, but she wrote out for herself, first, the full and truthful account of what she had done and what she had reported, so that the settlement resolved the matter without ever becoming the story she told herself about who she was.

How clean accountability makes you stronger

There is a counterintuitive truth at the heart of this chapter worth drawing out: owning your genuine mistake cleanly does not weaken your position against the false frame, it strengthens it. People trapped in all-or-nothing thinking assume that admitting anything hands the institution ammunition, and so they defend everything, including the indefensible, which is precisely what makes them look evasive and confirms the institution's picture of them as someone who will not take responsibility. The person who can say plainly, this specific thing was mine and I own it, and this sweeping frame was not, demonstrates the capacity for real accountability, which is the very thing the reversal is built to avoid, and which the institution itself has conspicuously failed to show.

This has a practical effect on how you are perceived and, more importantly, on how you perceive yourself. To any fair observer, a person who owns real faults and refuses false ones reads as truthful, while a person who denies everything reads as evasive, and the reversal actually benefits when you deny the true parts, because your obvious evasion on the real fault makes your denial of the false frame look equally unreliable. Clean accountability breaks that. And for your own recovery it matters even more, because owning what was genuinely yours is what lets you set it down. A fault that is faced and owned can be released; a fault that is denied festers, and a fault falsely inflated to include the institution's whole frame crushes. Sevrin found that owning the unauthorized access cleanly, far from proving the institution right, was what finally let her stop carrying both the real fault and the false frame, because the real had been handled and the false could now be clearly seen as separate.

Trying it on your own situation

Practice owning the part while refusing the frame, on real material.

First, return to your two lists and look hard at the first one, your genuine faults. For each, write a clean, specific ownership: this thing, which I did, was wrong. Notice that naming it precisely does not require accepting anything on the second list, the institution's false frame.

Second, for any accountability you genuinely owe, draft it in the clean form: the specific act named, responsibility taken without blame-shifting, nothing conceded beyond the actual fault. Read it aloud and listen for the two failure modes, the vague non-admission that owns nothing and the over-admission that spills past the act into accepting the frame, and keep it between them.

Third, write the sentence that holds both at once, your version of: I did this specific thing and it was wrong and I own it, and I reported a genuine wrong and was not the wrongdoer the institution describes. That sentence is the whole of this chapter, and it is the mature position the all-or-nothing trap says you cannot have.

Fourth, if you are offered a negotiated exit or settlement conditioned on accepting fault, write out your own truthful account first, before you weigh the offer. Set down plainly what you actually did and what you actually reported, and keep it. Then weigh the offer with proper advice as a practical decision, knowing that taking a resolution for practical reasons does not require you to believe the confession you may sign, and that a document signed under pressure must never become the account you tell yourself about your own life.

What to carry forward

For the reader who made a genuine mistake, the trap is all-or-nothing thinking, the belief that owning any fault concedes the institution's whole case, and the way out is to own the part and refuse the frame. A specific mistake, even a serious one, does not transform you into the wrongdoer or the wrongdoer into the victim, so admitting a real fault does not, in logic or truth, concede the false frame, however hard the reversal works to attach the whole story to the part by exploiting your conscience. Do genuine accountability cleanly, naming the specific act at its real size and stopping there, kept entirely separate from the false frame, and notice that owning a real fault cleanly makes you more credible, not less. Distinguish the mistake you own from the sweeping false confession the institution wants, especially in settlements and negotiated exits, where accepting a practical resolution need not mean believing the frame, and where you can hold and record the truth of what happened even as you resolve the matter (Neff, 2003). Having learned to own your part while refusing the frame, the next chapter takes up the defining decision that remains, whether to stay, leave, or pursue the matter further.

Chapter 12: Stay, Leave, or Pursue

Valenor stayed and pursued a grievance, and Éloane left and never looked back, and both of them made the right decision, because they made their own. Valenor was forty-nine and decided, after long thought and proper advice, to remain in his post and pursue a formal grievance and, eventually, an external complaint, because he judged that he could withstand the process and that the matter was worth the fight. Éloane was forty-six and decided, after her own long thought, that any further engagement with the institution would cost her more than she could afford, and she resigned, took a settlement, and built a life elsewhere. Neither decision was braver or wiser than the other. What made both of them right was that each person weighed their own values, their own safety, their own resources, and the realistic prospects, and reached a conclusion they could stand behind, rather than following a rule handed to them by a book, a forum, or a well-meaning friend. This chapter is about that decision, and about making it yours.

This chapter takes up the defining practical question for a reader in your situation: what to do about the institution that turned on you. Do you stay and try to remain, do you leave, or do you pursue the matter through grievance, legal action, a regulator, or an external body. Most advice on this pushes you in one direction: some of it says you must fight, that to leave is to let them win; some says you must get out, that to stay is to destroy yourself; some says just move on, that any pursuit is a waste of your life. None of this serves you, because none of it respects that this is your decision, based on your particular situation, your resources, and the realistic prospects. This chapter offers not a prescription but a framework: a way to decide, by your own values, safety, and circumstances, among the real options available to you.

The decision is yours to make

The principle of this chapter is that the decision is yours, to be made by your values, safety, and circumstances, not by anyone's rule. There is no correct answer that applies to every reader, because situations differ, institutions differ, resources differ, and what serves and protects one person would damage another. The options are real and legitimate: staying and remaining in place while protecting yourself, leaving on the best terms you can secure, and pursuing the matter through a grievance, a legal claim, a regulator, or another external body. None of these is inherently the right choice or the brave choice or the strong choice. The right choice is the one that, after careful thought and proper advice, best fits your values, keeps you safe, and reckons squarely with your resources and the realistic prospects, and only you can determine what that is.

This framing matters because the pressure on this decision comes from every direction, and most of it wants to make the choice for you. Some voices insist you must fight to the end, and treat leaving as surrender. Others insist you must protect yourself by leaving, and treat staying as self-destruction. Both are trying to hand you a rule, and both are wrong to, because a rule cannot know your situation, your finances, your health, your responsibilities, or the actual odds you face. Reclaiming this decision as yours, to be made deliberately rather than by pressure or slogan, is itself part of recovering from the reversal, because the institution treated you as an object to be managed, and deciding your own course by your own judgment is an act of the self-possession the whole book has been building toward.

Deciding by values, safety, and resources

To decide well, you weigh several things together, and they will pull in more than one direction, which is why the decision is hard. Your values matter: what you care about, whether the fight itself matters to you, whether staying or leaving fits the person you want to be. Your safety matters, including your psychological and physical health, because a fight that will destroy your wellbeing is a heavy price whatever the principle at stake. Your resources matter, the financial reserves, the time, the energy, the support a prolonged pursuit requires, because these fights are expensive in every currency and pretending otherwise helps no one. And the realistic prospects matter, the actual odds of the pursuit succeeding, which proper advice can help you assess, because staking everything on a fight you are very unlikely to win is a different decision from pursuing one with a real chance.

Holding these together with care is the work. A person who values the fight, has the resources to sustain it, and faces reasonable odds might rightly choose to pursue; a person for whom the cost to health and finances would be ruinous, or the odds vanishingly small, might rightly choose to leave and rebuild, and that is not surrender but a clear-eyed allocation of a life's limited resources. There is no shame in leaving a fight you cannot afford to win, and no glory in a pursuit that destroys you for a principle. The decision is not about which option is noblest in the abstract; it is about which fits your actual values, safety, resources, and prospects, weighed together and with proper advice. Éloane did not experience her decision to leave as defeat; she experienced it as a clear judgment that her health and her future were worth more than a fight she was unlikely to win against an institution with limitless resources.

Holding the guilt and the sunk cost

Whatever you decide, two feelings will press on the decision, and the task is to hold them without letting them decide: guilt and sunk cost. Guilt tells you that leaving means letting the institution win, letting the wrongdoing stand, abandoning others who might be harmed, and this guilt can push you to keep fighting past the point of wisdom. Sunk cost tells you that you have already invested so much, so much time and money and suffering, that you cannot stop now, and this too can trap you in a fight long after it has stopped being worth it. Both feelings are powerful, and neither is a reliable guide, because both push you to keep going regardless of whether continuing actually serves you.

This is why you cannot let guilt or sunk cost make the decision. The question is not what you have already spent or what leaving would mean symbolically; the question is what, from here, best serves your values, safety, resources, and prospects going forward. What you have already lost is gone whether you continue or not, and continuing a ruinous fight to honor a sunk cost only adds to the loss. Deciding by guilt hands your future to a feeling installed by a culture that treats leaving as failure; deciding by sunk cost hands it to a loss you cannot recover. Valenor chose to pursue his grievance, but he made the choice by weighing the prospects and his resources going forward, not by the guilt of stopping or the cost already spent, and that is why his decision to fight was as clear-eyed as Éloane's decision to leave.

When to bring in the professionals, and the two extremes met fairly

This decision, more than any other in the book, is one you should not make without proper professional advice, because it turns on legal and practical realities that a book cannot assess for your particular situation. A qualified lawyer or advocate can tell you your actual rights, the realistic odds, the likely costs, and the practical consequences of each option, and this information is essential to a sound decision. If your safety is genuinely at risk, that weighs heavily and may settle the matter, and it is a reason to seek appropriate help without delay. A book can give you a framework for weighing the decision; it cannot give you the specific legal and practical facts your decision requires, and seeking those out is part of deciding well.

It is also worth meeting the two extremes of advice fairly, because you will hear both. One says you must always fight, that to leave is to betray yourself and everyone the institution might harm next; the other says you should always just move on, that any pursuit is a self-destructive waste. Each contains a grain of truth and fails as a rule. It is true that fights sometimes matter beyond yourself and that leaving can leave a wrong unaddressed; it is also true that some pursuits destroy the person for little gain and that moving on can be the healthiest choice. The answer to both is the same: decide by a genuine weighing of your own values, safety, resources, and prospects, with proper advice, rather than by either slogan. A decision made that way is sound whichever way it goes, because it rests on your actual situation rather than on an ideology of fighting or of moving on. Between them, Valenor and Éloane made opposite choices, and both were right, because both were reached by careful weighing rather than by a rule.

The decision is not permanent

One thing that makes this decision feel unbearable is the sense that it is final, that choosing one path now forecloses the others forever, and it helps to know that this is often less true than it feels. Many of these decisions can be revisited as circumstances change. You might leave now and pursue a claim later, within the time limits the law allows. You might stay for a period to secure your position and leave when you are ready. You might pursue one avenue, find it costs too much, and choose to stop. Some options do have real deadlines, which is one more reason to get proper advice early, but the decision is generally a response to where things stand now, not an irreversible verdict for all time, and holding it that way makes it far less frightening to make.

This matters because the fear of permanence can push people into staying in a ruinous fight, on the reasoning that stopping would be forever and forever is too much to concede. But in many cases you are not choosing forever; you are choosing what serves you now, with some freedom to choose again as things change, provided you protect your options by getting timely advice about any deadlines. Éloane, who left, did not experience her decision as closing every door for all time; she left knowing she had preserved, on her lawyer's advice, the external avenues that remained open to her, and she chose later, from a place of stability, which of them if any to pursue, rather than deciding everything at once in the exhaustion of the moment.

Whichever you choose, protect the inner work

A final point ties this decision to the rest of the book: whichever path you choose, the inner work of the earlier chapters continues, and none of the three options substitutes for it. Staying does not require you to accept the institution's frame; you can remain in place while holding, privately and firmly, the truth of what happened and refusing the role assigned to you. Leaving does not resolve the reversal by itself; you can leave and still carry the self-doubt, the installed accuser, and the unhealed betrayal, which is why the rebuilding of the final chapter matters as much for those who go as for those who stay. And pursuing the matter does not deliver peace even if it succeeds, because vindication through a process, where it comes at all, does not automatically rebuild the self the reversal damaged.

This is worth holding because people sometimes treat the stay-leave-pursue decision as the whole of their recovery, as though choosing rightly among the three would resolve everything. It will not, on its own. The decision determines your external path; the inner work of understanding the reversal, weighing your own conduct fairly, holding your bearings, releasing the vindication you cannot control, tending your people, and rebuilding your self proceeds alongside whichever path you take. Both Valenor, who stayed and fought, and Éloane, who left, did the same inner work regardless of their opposite external choices, and both found that the inner work, not the external decision, was what finally freed them from the institution's account of who they were.

Trying it on your own situation

Make the decision your own.

First, name the real options for your situation: staying and remaining in place while protecting yourself, leaving on the best terms you can secure, or pursuing the matter through a grievance, a legal claim, a regulator, or another external body. Write what each would actually look like in practice, so you are choosing among real courses rather than abstractions.

Second, weigh your values, safety, resources, and the realistic prospects together, on paper and with proper advice. List what pulls in each direction plainly, including the financial and health costs and the actual odds, and reach a balance you can stand behind. Write down the decision and the reasons, so you can return to them when guilt or sunk cost presses.

Third, name the professional support the decision requires: the lawyer or advocate who can assess your rights and prospects, and, if your safety is in question, the service or authority you would contact. Deciding this in advance means the facts you need are within reach, and it keeps the hardest version of the decision from being one you face without proper guidance.

Fourth, frame the decision as a decision for now, not forever, and get early advice about any deadlines so you do not lose options by waiting. Note the current conditions your choice rests on and what would have to change for you to revisit it. And whichever path you choose, write down that the inner work continues regardless: staying, leaving, and pursuing each determine your external path, but none of them substitutes for understanding the reversal, holding your bearings, and rebuilding your self, which is the work the final chapter takes up.

What to carry forward

The decision to stay, leave, or pursue is yours, to be made by your values, safety, resources, and the realistic prospects rather than by any rule, because staying, leaving, and pursuing are all legitimate, and the right one is whichever best fits your situation after careful thought and proper advice. Weigh these together with care, accepting that they pull in more than one direction, and know that there is no shame in leaving a fight you cannot afford to win and no glory in a pursuit that destroys you. Hold the guilt and the sunk cost without letting them decide, because both push you to continue regardless of whether continuing serves you, and the real question is what best serves you going forward, not what you have already spent. Bring in proper legal and practical advice, since this decision turns on realities a book cannot assess, and meet the extremes of always fight and always move on not by either slogan but by a genuine weighing, which makes your decision sound whichever way it goes. Having made the decision that will shape your path, the final chapter turns to the deepest work, rebuilding a self and a life after the institution turned on you.

Chapter 13: Rebuilding After the Institution

Noélin rebuilt herself the way you rebuild after a fire: not by pretending the fire never happened, but by clearing the ground and building something new on it. She was forty-seven, and two years after the institution forced her out for reporting a senior colleague's misconduct, the deepest damage was not to her career, which she was slowly rebuilding, but to her sense of herself. She could not trust her own judgment anymore. When she considered raising a concern in her new job, a voice asked whether she was being a troublemaker again. When she felt sure about something, a voice asked whether she was as difficult and misguided as the institution had said. She had absorbed the institution's account so completely that she had become her own accuser, unable to act on her own perception without interrogating it for the fault the institution had taught her to assume was there. This chapter is about how she came back from that, and how you can, because rebuilding a self and a life after the institution turned on you is the deepest work in the book, and it is the point of everything that came before.

Everything so far has helped you understand the reversal, weigh your own conduct, respond to the process, release the vindication you cannot control, and decide about your path. This final chapter turns to the injury underneath all of it: the damage to your relationship with yourself and to the working life the institution took. Being turned on by an institution you trusted can install a self-doubt that operates for years, leaving you unable to trust your own judgment, and it can strip away a professional identity that was central to who you were. Rebuilding both, the self and the working life, is possible, and like all trust that has been broken, it is rebuilt not by insistence but by evidence, gathered patiently over time.

Rebuilding on evidence

The principle of this chapter is that self-trust is rebuilt by evidence, not by insistence. You cannot simply decide to trust your own judgment again, any more than you could decide to trust an institution that had betrayed you; the trust has to be earned back, even from yourself, through accumulated evidence of your actual character and competence. This is oddly hopeful, because it gives you something to do other than wait for the feeling to change. You gather evidence. You notice, and record, the moments when your conduct and judgment prove sound, until the weight of that accumulated evidence begins to outweigh the institution's account, and your trust in yourself is rebuilt on a foundation of observed fact rather than on either the institution's verdict or a forced positive thinking that never quite convinces.

This approach works where insistence fails because it engages the very faculty the reversal corrupted: your capacity to judge your own character and competence from evidence. The institution did not just assert you were the problem; it trained you to read your own judgment as suspect, so that even your sound instincts came to feel like troublemaking. Rebuilding trust by evidence retrains that faculty in the other direction, teaching you to read your conduct and judgment accurately again. It is slow, because trust is always slow to rebuild, but it is reliable, because it is grounded in what you actually do rather than in what you or anyone else asserts about you.

The accuser the institution installed

The particular difficulty many people face is that they have absorbed the institution's accusing account so completely that they now do the accusing themselves, interrogating their own judgment for the fault they were taught to assume. Recovery here begins with recognizing this internalized accuser as a foreign installation, not your own judgment, and declining to accept its authority. When the voice asks whether you are being a troublemaker again, whether your concern is as misguided as the institution said, you learn to notice it, name it as the installed accuser rather than your conscience, and refuse to treat its interrogation as legitimate. Recovery from harm of this kind involves, in part, reclaiming authority over your own inner life from the account that colonized it (Herman, 1992).

This is not a single act but a practice, repeated over months, of catching the internalized accuser and refusing its authority, until it quiets for lack of agreement. Alongside the refusal, there is a gentler move that is just as important: meeting yourself with the care you would offer a colleague who had been through what you have been through. Harsh self-attack, the mode the institution trained into you, keeps you locked in the accuser's frame; self-compassion, treating yourself with the ordinary kindness you would extend to anyone who had suffered this, loosens that frame and creates room for a truer self-assessment (Neff, 2003). You are not indulging yourself by being kind to yourself; you are refusing the institution's method, which was to make you your own prosecutor, and replacing it with the care that actually allows accurate sight.

Anger, grief, and the body

Two emotional currents usually need to move as part of this rebuilding, and both are easy to block. The first is anger, appropriate anger, at what was done to you. Many people turned on by an institution suppress their anger, either because expressing it during the process would have been used against them or because they have absorbed the idea that their anger is the very thing that proves them difficult. But the legitimate outrage of a person who reported a wrong and was punished for it is healthy, and reclaiming it, without acting on it destructively, is part of recovering a self that knows it was wronged. This anger is not the dangerous force the institution called it; it is the signal that a real injustice occurred, and letting yourself feel it is part of coming back.

The second current is grief, because there is a great deal to mourn: the career or standing the institution took, the colleagues and community lost, the faith in institutions that is gone, the years the ordeal consumed, the version of your life that would have continued had you never reported. Recovery includes mourning these losses rather than rushing past them, because grief that is felt can move through and settle, while grief that is denied stays lodged and blocks the recovery behind it (Herman, 1992). Letting yourself grieve what the reversal cost you is not self-pity; it is the honoring of real and serious losses, and it is part of how you come out the other side. And because sustained stress of this kind is held in the body as much as the mind, this anger and grief often need to move through the body as well, at your own pace and frequently with skilled help, as part of the physical work of recovery (van der Kolk, 2014).

Rebuilding the working life, and when to get help

Beyond the self, there is often a working life to rebuild, and this deserves its own word, because the practical loss can feel as large as the psychological one. Being forced out or pushed aside can take not only a job but a profession, a network, a standing built over years, and rebuilding a working life after that is real and sometimes long work. It may mean a new role, a new field, a new place, or a changed relationship to work altogether, and there is no single right shape for it. What matters is that a working life can be rebuilt, often on ground that turns out to be sturdier than the institution that failed you, and that the person who rebuilds it is frequently not the same as the one who was pushed out, but someone who has learned to hold their own judgment and to see institutions clearly, which are not small gains.

This rebuilding, of the self and the working life both, is often work that benefits from skilled help, and there is no failure in needing it. A good therapist can help you distinguish the installed accuser from your own judgment, hold the anger and grief without being overwhelmed, and rebuild self-trust in a supported way that is hard to achieve by yourself. This is especially so if you are experiencing symptoms that interfere with daily functioning, such as persistent inability to sleep, pervasive hopelessness, or thoughts of harming yourself, any of which is a clear reason to reach for professional help without delay. Reaching for that help is not evidence that you are as damaged as the institution claimed; it is evidence that you are taking your own recovery seriously, which is exactly what a person worth trusting does. Noélin worked with a therapist through her rebuilding, and found that having help to separate the installed accuser from her own judgment was what finally let her raise a concern in her new job without the old voice convincing her she was a troublemaker, which was the moment she knew she had come back.

The self that reported was not wrong to report

There is a particular knot in this rebuilding that deserves direct attention, because it can quietly poison a recovery: the temptation to conclude that the whole thing was your fault for reporting, that if you had only stayed silent none of this would have happened, and therefore that the lesson is never to speak up again. This conclusion is understandable, because the cost of reporting was enormous, and the mind reaches for a way to prevent such pain in future. But it is the wrong lesson, and absorbing it hands the institution a final victory, teaching you to become the silent, compliant person the reversal was designed to produce.

The truer reckoning is that you were not wrong to report a real wrong; the institution was wrong to punish you for it. The pain you suffered was caused by the institution's betrayal, not by your decision to speak, and collapsing the two, blaming your reporting for the institution's reprisal, is a subtle form of accepting the reversal, because it relocates the fault from the institution back onto you. You can hold, at the same time, that reporting cost you dearly and that reporting was not the wrong you should learn to avoid. What you may sensibly learn is to be wiser about how and to whom you report, to get advice earlier, to protect yourself better; what you should not learn is that speaking up was itself the error. Noélin came, in time, to a clear position: that she would report again if she had to, though she would do it more carefully and with more protection, because the alternative, becoming a person who watched wrongdoing in silence, was a worse fate than the one the institution had inflicted, and she would not let the institution make her into that.

A slow return, and a different strength

A word about pace, because impatience with recovery is itself a way the reversal keeps its grip. Self-trust that took a prolonged betrayal to damage does not return in weeks, and the slowness can feel like failure, like proof that the institution's account was accurate or that you will never be sound again. It is neither. Rebuilding trust with yourself follows the same slow logic as rebuilding trust with anyone: it accumulates through repeated evidence over time, and cannot be rushed by force of will. The days when the self-doubt returns in full are not relapses that erase your progress; they are the ordinary texture of a long recovery, and they grow fewer and less total as the evidence accumulates. Measure your recovery not by whether the doubt has vanished, but by whether the record of your real character and competence is growing and whether, over months, you are a little more able to trust your own judgment when it and the old accuser disagree.

And there is a different strength on the far side of this, worth naming as something to move toward. The person who rebuilds after an institutional betrayal is often not restored to exactly who they were, but becomes someone harder to reverse: someone who understands how institutions behave, who reads power rather than politeness, who holds their own judgment against an official account, and who can no longer be so easily made to doubt themselves. That is not the innocence you had before, and its loss is a real grief, but it is a durable and clear-eyed strength, and it is yours. Noélin did not become again the person who had trusted the institution without reservation; she became someone steadier and less deceivable, who could act on her own judgment in a world she now saw more clearly, and who knew, from evidence, that she had reported a real wrong and survived being turned into the villain for it.

Trying it on your own situation

Begin rebuilding the self and the working life, on evidence, patiently.

First, start a record of your real character and competence: small, specific moments when your judgment proved sound, your conduct was decent, your work was good. Add to it regularly. You are gathering the evidence that will, over time, outweigh the institution's account.

Second, when the internalized accuser questions your judgment, practice naming it and declining its authority: that is the installed accuser, not my judgment, and I do not accept its interrogation. Pair the refusal with a kinder self-assessment, the one you would offer a colleague who had been through this.

Third, let one blocked emotion move this week, safely: allow yourself the appropriate anger at what was done, or the grief for the working life and community you lost, ideally with a trusted person or a professional alongside you. Feeling what was frozen is part of coming back to yourself.

Fourth, refuse the lesson that you were wrong to report. Write down the truer reckoning in your own words: that reporting a real wrong cost you dearly, and that the cost was caused by the institution's betrayal, not by your decision to speak. You may sensibly resolve to report more carefully and with more protection in future; do not resolve to become the silent person the reversal was designed to produce. Measuring your recovery by the growth of your record and your returning judgment, rather than by whether the doubt is gone, keeps the ordinary slowness of coming back from being read as failure.

A closing word, and it is the one this chapter has been moving toward. You reported a wrong, and the institution turned on you, and for a long while, perhaps still, it made you doubt whether you should have spoken and whether you were the problem after all. The work of rebuilding is slow and it is real and it is yours to do, one accurate observation at a time, with help where you need it and patience always. The institution was powerful, and its account got inside you, and it tried to convince you that your own judgment could not be trusted. It was wrong. You can rebuild a self you rely on and a life worth living, grounded in the evidence of who you actually are, and when you have, the institution's account will have lost the only power it ever truly held over you, which was your agreement.

What to carry forward

Self-trust is rebuilt not by insistence but by evidence, gathered patiently until the weight of your actual character and competence outweighs the institution's account and you can rely on your own judgment again. Recover authority over your inner life from the internalized accuser by naming it as a foreign installation rather than your conscience, and pair that refusal with self-compassion, since harsh self-attack keeps you in the accuser's frame while kindness allows accurate sight (Herman, 1992; Neff, 2003). Let your appropriate anger and your genuine grief move rather than blocking them, because felt emotion settles while denied emotion stays lodged, and this work often needs to move through the body with skilled help (van der Kolk, 2014). Rebuild the working life as well as the self, knowing it can be rebuilt on sturdier ground, and bring in a professional for the deep work without shame, especially if daily functioning is affected. Rebuilding a self and a life after the institution turned on you, one accurate observation at a time, is the point of everything this book has done, and the conclusion gathers it all into the single truth the whole book has been for.

Conclusion: The Institution Was Not the Truth

At the start of this book, you wrote down two things: the wrong you reported, and the way the institution turned it into a case against you. Find those now, at the end, and read them again, because you are a different reader than the one who wrote them. When you wrote them, the institution's turning may have felt like a verdict, something true and damning about who you are. I hope that by now it reads differently, as what it actually is: a system protecting itself, a reversal aimed at the person who named a wrong, examined by you and found not to be the truth. The words on the page have not changed. You have.

That is the whole movement of this book, from a person defined by the institution's account to a person who understands the reversal, knows their own conduct and character, and is no longer ruled by what the institution said. We began by seeing that the depth of the betrayal came from the depth of your dependence, and that the institution recast you from reporter to accused through the same tactic of deny, attack, and reverse. We faced the question of whether you got it wrong, and answered it not with reassurance but with a fair self-check that owns what is real and refuses what is false. We learned that your record is the ground you stand on against the institution's rewriting, and that an institution is read by the direction of its power rather than the politeness of its process.

From there the work turned outward and then back in. We prepared for colleagues and committees closing ranks, and learned to stay steady when the community turned. We learned to answer the process calmly and on the record, and to release the vindication that so rarely comes. We turned toward the people who still stand with you, we learned to survive the prolonged ordeal by tending body and mind, and we learned to own any genuine mistake while refusing the institution's frame. We made a clear, values-based decision about whether to stay, leave, or pursue. And we turned to the deepest work, rebuilding the self and the working life the institution damaged, on the evidence of who you actually are.

Underneath all of it has been a single truth, the one this conclusion is here to state plainly: the institution's account was not the truth. It was a system defending itself, and its turning on you was a report on the institution, not on your worth or your judgment or your character. The reversal that recast you as the problem depends for its power on two things, your self-doubt and the absence of any clear account of what really happened. You have taken both away from it. You have replaced the self-doubt with a grounded conclusion reached by fair examination, and you have replaced the absence of an account with a clear record and a growing store of evidence about who you actually are. Stripped of those two supports, the institution's account loses its hold, not because the institution stops asserting it, but because you have stopped supplying the agreement it needed.

There is a freedom in this that does not depend on anything you cannot control. You may never be vindicated. The institution may never admit what it did, the people who turned may never come around, the wrong you reported may never be addressed, the account may stand on the record for the rest of your life. And you can be free anyway, because the freedom this book has been building was never the freedom of being cleared by the institution. It was the freedom of knowing, on the evidence, who you actually are and what actually happened, and no longer needing the institution's admission to hold that knowledge steady. That freedom cannot be withheld from you by anyone, because you build it and you keep it, out of courage and a fair method and the patient accumulation of evidence.

So carry your conclusion, keep your record, tend the people who stand with you and the community you are building, and walk on.

Read your record when the institution's account resurfaces in your mind, and let it hold you until the moment passes, which it will, more quickly each time. Be patient with the slow return of trust in your own judgment, and reach for help when you need it, without shame. And when the old voice comes to tell you that you were the problem, that you should have stayed silent, that the institution was right about you, meet it with the truth you have earned: that you reported a real wrong, that you were right to do so, that you owned what was genuinely yours and refused what was not, and that the institution's turning on you was its failure and not your fault. You turned to them for help, and they turned on you. That was never the measure of who you are. You are the person who saw the reversal for what it was, kept your bearings, and came back to a self you can trust, in a world you now see clearly. The institution was not the truth. You were. Name the tactic. Reclaim your story. The rest of your life is waiting, and it is yours.

Appendix A: The Did I Get This Wrong Self-Check

This self-check gathers the questions from Chapter 3 into one place, so you can return to it whenever the doubt resurfaces. It is not a diagnostic instrument and it cannot determine the facts of your situation. It is a structured way to examine your own conduct fairly, and its value depends entirely on your willingness to answer in good faith rather than to reach a predetermined verdict in either direction. Work through it slowly, in writing, ideally more than once and ideally with a trusted person or a professional alongside you.

First, the willingness question. Are you willing to consider that you might have been mistaken, or that you handled the reporting badly. Someone who reported in genuine bad faith is characteristically untroubled by this question, so the very fact that you are asking it in good faith already distinguishes you from the reckless accuser the institution describes. Notice your willingness, and notice too any impulse to convict yourself of everything, which is its own kind of avoidance.

Second, the basis question. What exactly did you report, and what was your basis for it. Write down the specific facts you had, the evidence you relied on, and the reasonable grounds for your concern, setting aside the institution's later characterization of your motives.

Third, the good-faith question. Did you report in good faith, on reasonable grounds, believing the concern was real and worth raising. A genuine concern reported in good faith is not wrongdoing even if you turned out to be mistaken about some detail, and this question separates a good-faith report from a reckless or malicious one.

Fourth, the conduct question. Setting aside whether the concern was valid, was there something in how you handled it that you genuinely regret: a way you communicated, a step you skipped, a line you crossed. Answer this specifically, in terms of particular actions, not sweeping self-condemnation.

Fifth, the proportion question. Looking at the whole, is the institution's response proportionate to any error you actually made, or wildly out of proportion. A response far out of proportion to any real error is itself a strong sign of a reversal rather than a fair correction.

Having worked through these, write two lists. The first is the genuine faults, the specific things you actually got wrong or handled badly, which you will own and, where appropriate, repair. The second is the false frame, the sweeping characterization of you as reckless, malicious, or the real problem, which you will refuse. Keep them strictly separate. If some items stay genuinely unclear, list them separately and let them be unclear, rather than defaulting to the institution's verdict.

Appendix B: Institutional Betrayal or a Fair Process

This guide gathers the discernment tools from Chapters 1 and 5 for telling institutional betrayal from a genuinely fair process. It is meant to help a genuine reporter read their situation clearly. It is not a way to dismiss every unwelcome outcome as betrayal, and if a fair reading shows the process was sound and the finding warranted, that is worth knowing too.

Consider direction. Across the whole matter, not in single steps, whom does the process protect and whom does it disadvantage. A fair process is willing to find against the institution and its powerful members; a captured one consistently protects them and disadvantages the reporter.

Consider control. Who runs the process, and are they genuinely independent of the institution, or are their careers, loyalties, and incentives bound up with it. A review is only as independent as its terms, its reporting lines, and its incentives allow, whatever label is attached to it.

Consider proportion. Is the response to your report and your conduct proportionate, or wildly out of scale. An institution that responds to a good-faith report with an overwhelming reprisal is showing the reversal at work.

Consider the subject. Has the process kept its focus on the wrong you reported, or has it shifted to become an inquiry into you, your credibility, your character, your conduct. A shift of subject from the wrong to the reporter is a signature of the reversal.

A caution, kept deliberately in view: not every unwelcome finding is betrayal, and a fair process can reach a conclusion you dislike. If a genuinely independent process, focused on the right subject and proportionate in its response, finds against you on reasonable grounds, that is a different situation from the reversal this book describes, and the truthful response to it is the accountability of Chapter 11, not a search for betrayal where there was none.

Appendix C: The Documentation and Response Template

This template gathers the record-keeping and response disciplines from Chapters 4 and 7. Its logic is simple: keep a stable record the institution cannot rewrite, and answer the process narrowly, factually, and on the record.

For the record. Write things down as close to the time as possible, because contemporaneous notes are more accurate and more stabilizing than memory recalled later. Record specifics: dates, times, who was present, what was said, in plain factual language rather than interpretation. Preserve the documents you already have, and keep your record in your own private space, not on a system the institution controls. Keep your documentation lawful and within your rights, and where retaining or recording certain material raises legal questions, take proper advice.

For responses. Before responding at all, wait, and do not respond while activated. Answer only the specific, answerable points, factually and on the record. Decline the character attack entirely, because it is not a question but a hook. Keep important exchanges in writing where you can, and follow up meetings with your own written account of what was discussed.

The third reader. Before you send anything, imagine that a fair, impartial outside reader will one day read it, and write so that this reader would see a calm, factual, reasonable person. This strips out the heat, the counter-attacks, and the pleading, leaving only what serves you.

The feeling goes elsewhere. Write the furious reply if you need to, and do not send it. Take the real emotional pressure to a trusted person, an advocate, a therapist, or a private page, so the record stays measured while your feeling is fully honored somewhere it can do some good.

Appendix D: Genuine Mistake or False Confession

This guide gathers the distinction from Chapter 11, for readers who made a genuine mistake and need to own it without accepting the institution's frame. Use it to tell an accountability you should offer from a confession the reversal wants to extract.

Genuine accountability is specific: it names a real, identifiable act. False confession is sweeping: it admits that you were the wrongdoer or that the wrong you reported was not real.

Genuine accountability is proportionate: it owns the actual fault at its actual size. False confession is inflated: it accepts responsibility for far more than you did, up to the institution's whole frame.

Genuine accountability is freely given: it comes from your own conscience. False confession is extracted: it is produced under pressure, often as a condition of a settlement, a resignation, or an end to the process.

Genuine accountability is true: you did the thing you are owning. False confession is false: you are admitting to being the wrongdoer when you reported a genuine wrong.

The practical rule is to keep your two lists in view and let each guide the right response. The first list, your genuine faults, is where accountability belongs; make it fully and specifically. The second list, the false frame, is where refusal belongs; decline it as firmly as you own the first, however strongly you are told that real accountability requires accepting it. And where a settlement or exit requires you to sign something, weigh it with proper advice, and know that taking a practical resolution need not mean believing the confession, and that a document signed under pressure must never become the account you tell yourself about your own life.

Appendix E: The Stay, Leave, or Pursue Worksheet

This worksheet gathers the framework from Chapter 12. It does not tell you what to decide. It gives you a structured way to decide by your own values, safety, resources, and the realistic prospects, and it is not a substitute for proper legal and practical advice.

Name the real options for your situation, and write what each would actually look like in practice: staying and remaining in place while protecting yourself; leaving on the best terms you can secure; or pursuing the matter through a grievance, a legal claim, a regulator, or another external body.

Weigh your values. What do you care about here. Does the fight itself matter to you. Which path fits the person you want to be. Notice that your values may pull in more than one direction.

Weigh your safety and your resources. What would each path cost your health, your finances, your time, and your energy. There is no shame in declining a fight you cannot afford to win, and no glory in a pursuit that destroys you.

Weigh the realistic prospects. With proper advice, what are the actual odds of a pursuit succeeding, and what are the real consequences of each option. Staking everything on a fight you are very unlikely to win is a different decision from pursuing one with a real chance.

Hold the guilt and the sunk cost without letting them decide. Both push you to continue regardless of whether continuing serves you. The real question is what best serves you going forward, not what leaving would symbolize or what you have already spent.

Frame it as a decision for now, not forever, and get early advice about any deadlines so you do not lose options by waiting. Name the professional support you will draw on whichever way you choose.

Appendix F: A Record of Your Real Standing

This appendix supports the practice from Chapter 13, of rebuilding self-trust on evidence. Its premise is that self-trust returns not through insistence but through the patient accumulation of accurate observations of your actual character and competence, gathered until their weight outbalances the institution's account.

Keep an ongoing record. It can be a notebook, a note on your phone, a document, anything you will actually use. Into it, regularly, put small, specific, true observations of your own conduct, judgment, and work: a moment your judgment proved sound, a time you acted with decency under pressure, an instance of good work or fair dealing. Specific and true is the whole point; this is not positive thinking, which the installed accuser easily dismisses, but a record of real evidence it cannot fairly wave away.

When the internalized accuser questions your judgment, turning your sound instincts into troublemaking and your competence into a liability, bring it to the record. Set its sweeping claim against the specific accumulated evidence of how you actually conduct yourself and how well you actually work. Over months, the weight of accurate observation begins to shift which voice you believe, not by argument but by evidence, until you can once again rely on your own judgment.

Add to the record on good days and bad. On the bad days, when the institution's account feels true, the record is there precisely to be read, a store of evidence gathered in clearer moments and kept ready for the moments you cannot see yourself accurately. This is how a self is rebuilt after an institutional betrayal: one true observation at a time, patiently, until the person on the page and the person you feel yourself to be become, at last, the same.

Appendix G: The DARVO Survival Guides

This book is part of a series that examines DARVO, the reversal tactic in which a person or a body confronted with wrongdoing, or simply resisted, responds by denying it, attacking the one who named it, and reversing the roles of victim and offender so that the person who was harmed is blamed as the offender. Each book in the series applies this lens to a different situation, and each can be read on its own or alongside the others.

The companion volumes develop, in their own contexts, several tools this book draws on: the fair self-check, the practice of writing for a third reader, the reading of a situation by power and direction rather than by appearances, and the discipline of keeping your own record. Readers facing the reversal in an adult relationship, a friendship, a divorce or custody dispute, or the family of origin will find those situations addressed directly in the companion volumes. This volume turns to the reversal at the level of the institution, when a body you depended on protects itself by turning on the person who reported a wrong.

If this book served you, the most useful thing you can do, beyond applying it, is to leave a truthful review where you bought it, so that others in the same painful situation can find it. Being turned on by an institution you trusted is an isolating experience, and many who go through it do not know there is a name for what happened to them or a way through it. A review is how the next person finds the door.

Name the tactic. Reclaim your story.

References

Baumeister, R. F., Bratslavsky, E., Finkenauer, C., & Vohs, K. D. (2001). Bad is stronger than good. *Review of General Psychology, 5*(4), 323-370. https://doi.org/10.1037/1089-2680.5.4.323

Freyd, J. J. (1996). *Betrayal trauma: The logic of forgetting childhood abuse.* Harvard University Press.

Freyd, J. J. (1997). Violations of power, adaptive blindness, and betrayal trauma theory. *Feminism & Psychology, 7*(1), 22-32. https://doi.org/10.1177/0959353597071004

Harsey, S. J., & Freyd, J. J. (2020). Deny, attack, and reverse victim and offender (DARVO): What is the influence on perceived perpetrator and victim credibility? *Journal of Aggression, Maltreatment & Trauma, 29*(8), 897-916. https://doi.org/10.1080/10926771.2020.1774695

Harsey, S. J., Zurbriggen, E. L., & Freyd, J. J. (2017). Perpetrator responses to victim confrontation: DARVO and victim self-blame. *Journal of Aggression, Maltreatment & Trauma, 26*(6), 644-663. https://doi.org/10.1080/10926771.2017.1320777

Herman, J. L. (1992). *Trauma and recovery.* Basic Books.

Neff, K. D. (2003). Self-compassion: An alternative conceptualization of a healthy attitude toward oneself. *Self and Identity, 2*(2), 85-101. https://doi.org/10.1080/15298860309032

Porges, S. W. (2011). *The polyvagal theory: Neurophysiological foundations of emotions, attachment, communication, and self-regulation.* W. W. Norton.

Smith, C. P., & Freyd, J. J. (2014). Institutional betrayal. *American Psychologist, 69*(6), 575-587. https://doi.org/10.1037/a0037564

Stark, E. (2007). *Coercive control: How men entrap women in personal life.* Oxford University Press.

Sweet, P. L. (2019). The sociology of gaslighting. *American Sociological Review, 84*(5), 851-875. https://doi.org/10.1177/0003122419874843

van der Kolk, B. A. (2014). *The body keeps the score: Brain, mind, and body in the healing of trauma.* Viking.

About the Author

Arnold Wellington McLean is a mental health professional and researcher with an interest in trauma. He writes about coercive relationships, family systems, institutions, and recovery, with a focus on turning current research into clear, practical guidance that ordinary readers can use. Reported, Then Blamed is the fifth book in The DARVO Survival Guides.

www.ingramcontent.com/pod-product-compliance
Lightning Source LLC
LaVergne TN
LVHW050824061126
851857LV00012B/960
* 9 7 9 8 9 0 6 7 8 1 9 8 7 *